The Team That History Forgot

The TEAM THAT HISTORY FORGOT

The 1960s Kansas City Chiefs

Rick Gosselin

Foreword by Andy Reid

University of Nebraska Press Lincoln

All images are courtesy of the Kansas City Chiefs archives.

Manufactured in the United States of America

The University of Nebraska Press is part of a land-grant institution with campuses and programs on the past, present, and future homelands of the Pawnee, Ponca, Otoe-Missouria, Omaha, Dakota, Lakota, Kaw, Cheyenne, and Arapaho Peoples, as well as those of the relocated Ho-Chunk, Sac and Fox, and Iowa Peoples.

For customers in the EU with safety/GPSR concerns, contact:
gpsr@mare-nostrum.co.uk
Mare Nostrum Group BV
Mauritskade 21D
1091 GC Amsterdam
The Netherlands

Library of Congress Cataloging-in-Publication Data
Names: Gosselin, Rick author |
Reid, Andy, 1958– author of foreword
Title: The team that history forgot: the 1960s Kansas City Chiefs / Rick Gosselin; foreword by Andy Reid.
Other titles: Nineteen sixties Kansas City Chiefs
Description: Lincoln: University of Nebraska Press, [2025] | Includes index.
Identifiers: LCCN 2025019691
ISBN 9781496243102 cloth acid-free paper
ISBN 9781496244741 epub
ISBN 9781496244758 pdf
Subjects: LCSH: Kansas City Chiefs (Football team)—History—20th century | Super Bowl—History—20th century
BISAC: SPORTS & RECREATION / Football | HISTORY / United States / State & Local / Midwest (IA, IL, IN, KS, MI, MN, MO, ND, NE, OH, SD, WI)
Classification: LCC GV956.K35 G67 2025 |
DDC 796.332/6409778411—dc23/eng/20250804
LC record available at https://lccn.loc.gov/2025019691

Designed and set in Lyon Text by L. Welch.

To Ellen,
the love of my life

Contents

Illustrations

Foreword

ANDY REID

Len Dawson and the Chiefs introduced the "choir huddle" during their days in the AFL. We brought it back for a play to open our preseason finale at Arrowhead in 2022.

We did it as a tribute to Dawson, who passed away days earlier, and the championship roots of this franchise. I have a deep appreciation for the history of the game of football. To know where you are going is to know where you are from.

I grew up in Los Angeles as a young fan of the Rams. I saw gridiron greatness there in the form of coach George Allen and the Fearsome Foursome, which featured Hall of Famers Deacon Jones and Merlin Olsen. I played my college football at BYU, which had its own history of success with coach LaVell Edwards.

My first job in the NFL was as an assistant offensive line coach in Green Bay. Talk about history! Lambeau Field, Vince Lombardi, Bart Starr, the power sweep. Every day there was a history lesson. My first opportunity as a head coach was with the Philadelphia Eagles. Another franchise steeped in history: Steve Van Buren, Norm Van Brocklin, Chuck Bednarik, Franklin Field, Dick Vermeil, The Vet . . .

Then I was fortunate to be hired by the Hunt family and the Chiefs as their head coach in 2013. The history of this franchise, and the American Football League for that matter, ooze at Arrowhead Stadium. The founding father of the Chiefs, Lamar Hunt, was also the founding father of the AFL. Lamar owned the league's flagship franchise, the Dallas Texans, and relocated the team to Kansas City as the Chiefs in 1963. Kansas City became the first AFL team to play in the Super Bowl and the last AFL team to win a Super Bowl.

Some of the greatest players in the game's history wore the arrowhead on their helmet—Dawson, Buck Buchanan, Johnny Robinson, Bobby Bell, Willie Lanier, Emmitt Thomas, Otis Taylor, Jan Stenerud . . . Lamar passed away in 2006 but entrusted the franchise—and both the history and traditions of this franchise—to his children Clark, Daniel, Sharon, and Lamar Jr. As our CEO, Clark has done a masterful job handling those responsibilities.

We still play in the same stadium that Lamar Hunt built and Dawson once played. Arrowhead remains one of the greatest venues for football with as rabid a fan base as you'll find anywhere. The AFL-era Chiefs taught Kansas City what winning football looks like—what *championship* football looks like—and our fan base continues to embrace that standard today. There is an expectation of winning. As a franchise, we owe so much to Lamar Hunt, Len Dawson, and the Chiefs of the AFL era. They planted the seeds for the Chiefs Kingdom.

Dawson continued to have a presence in Kansas City well after his Hall of Fame career ended in 1976. He was a longtime sports director at a local television station and also spent decades as the color commentator on the radio broadcast for our games. I think he would have appreciated Patrick Mahomes addressing our offense in the choir huddle that August night in 2022.

Rick Gosselin was absolutely the perfect choice for this book. He is a Hall of Fame writer with ties to Kansas City. He knows football, and he knows this franchise. He also has an appreciation for history. I've known Rick for decades, and his passion for this project can be seen in every page of this book. He ties the franchise's two championship eras together.

Andy Reid

Head Coach, Kansas City Chiefs

Andy Reid has coached the Kansas City Chiefs for twelve seasons. He has posted twelve consecutive winning seasons, qualifying for the playoffs eleven times and winning nine consecutive AFC West titles. He has coached the Chiefs to seven consecutive AFC championship games and five Super Bowls, winning three Lombardi Trophies. Reid previously spent fourteen seasons coaching the Philadelphia Eagles and also took them to a Super Bowl. In his twenty-six seasons as an NFL head coach, Reid has won 273 games—fourth most all-time behind Hall of Famers Don Shula, George Halas, and Bill Belichick.

The Team That History Forgot

Introduction

The Kansas City Chiefs are the best franchise in the NFL. They have played in seven consecutive AFC championship games and five Super Bowls, claiming three Lombardi Trophies. They have seized the NFL's dynasty mantle from the New England Patriots.

But dynasties are nothing new to Kansas City. Before there was Clark Hunt, there was Lamar Hunt. Before there was Andy Reid, there was Hank Stram. Before there was Patrick Mahomes, there was Len Dawson. Before there was Travis Kelce, there was Fred Arbanas. Before there was Chris Jones, there was Buck Buchanan. The Kansas City Chiefs of the 1960s were an AFL dynasty, also winning three championships in the decade.

I came to appreciate the AFL Chiefs long before the NFL Chiefs started winning Super Bowls.

Growing up in the 1960s in Grosse Pointe Park, a leafy suburb on the East side of Detroit, we neighborhood kids lived on the playground of Trombly Elementary School.

Wiffle ball on the front yard in the spring, baseball on the diamond in the summer, football on the grassy expanse behind the school in the fall—whatever the season, whatever the sport, we were playing. The touch football games were the most fun and often the most competitive. You could play them with as many as six players a side or as few as two.

I have vivid memories of the four-player games because they occasionally involved my older brother Tom. He and his best friend Mark Michael would play me and my best friend Danny Setter. We would always be the hometown Detroit Lions. We'd pretend to be Nick Pietrosante or Night Train Lane or Gail Cogdill or Joe Schmidt. On rare occasions we'd be the Green Bay Packers.

Tom and Mark were older than Danny and I by two years and, to our torment, would always claim to be an AFL team. They'd be the Kansas City Chiefs or the New York Jets or the San Diego Chargers . . . Len Dawson or Don Maynard or Lance Alworth . . . *Bambi*. And they would beat us every time. Which galled us. The AFL was inferior to the NFL. Everyone knew that. We were letting our league down.

Which is why I cheered for the Packers in the first two Super Bowls, the Colts in the third Super Bowl, and the Vikings in the fourth Super Bowl. They needed to uphold the dignity of the NFL, something that Danny and I failed to do at Trombly.

Now fast forward a decade and a half to 1977. I was a sports writer with *United Press International* and transferred from New York City to Kansas City to become the wire service's Midlands sports editor. One of the teams on my new beat was the Kansas City Chiefs.

Hanging out at Arrowhead Stadium, attending games and team functions, I got to know Lamar Hunt, who founded both the AFL and the Chiefs, and his family. I got to know Dawson, who became a local sportscaster in Kansas City. I got to know Otis Taylor, who became a scout for the Chiefs.

I got to know Johnny Robinson, Bobby Bell, Ed Budde, Buchanan, and Arbanas, who all played in the first Super Bowl loss to the Green Bay Packers. I got to know Willie Lanier, Jan Stenerud, Emmitt Thomas, and Jim Lynch, who all played in the Super Bowl IV victory over the Minnesota Vikings.

I found the old Chiefs all approachable, friendly, and likable. I always thought Kansas City was one of the best-kept secrets in America, and these men all embraced their small-market culture. All were generous with their time and memories. And as I delved into the history of the Chiefs, I came to appreciate and greatly respect these players, their team, and their accomplishments. The Kansas City Chiefs—and the AFL—were far better than I had ever given them credit for being.

I had the pleasure of covering Kansas City games at the close of the careers of Lanier, Lynch, Stenerud, and Thomas. I also served on the Pro Football Hall of Fame selection committee when Buchanan, Curley Culp, Robinson, Stenerud, and Thomas were enshrined in Canton. In fact, I made the presentations to the full committee for all five of those Chiefs.

In my career I covered the rise and rapid demise of other professional leagues—the World Football League (WFL), World Hockey Association (WHA), and the United States Football League (USFL)—and it always intrigued me how the AFL not only managed to survive but thrive. So during the thirteen years I spent roaming Arrowhead Stadium and the fifty years I spent covering the NFL, I visited with Hank Stram, Al Davis, Ralph Wilson, Sid Gillman, Lance Alworth, Gene Upshaw, Marty Schottenheimer, John Hadl, George Saimes, Tom Flores, and a host of other legendary AFL figures for their perspective on Lamar Hunt's league.

That first Super Bowl had been of particular interest to me. I remember watching it on a black-and-white television as a sixteen-year-old. Volumes have been written about Vince Lombardi, the Green Bay dynasty of the 1960s, and those first two Super Bowls. But little had been written about the team that lost the first Super Bowl—and the revenge tour that followed. The book had been in my notebook for four decades before I finally decided to put words to paper in 2023.

The backbone of this book is interviews conducted thirty and forty years ago when I was covering the Chiefs. Many of the subjects I had on tape or in my notebook have since passed away—Hunt, Dawson, Buchanan, Taylor, Budde, Arbanas, Walt Corey—but their memories and words live on in this story. I also had a couple of lengthy sit-downs with Hall of Fame maverick Al Davis, who was as colorful as he was insightful. He, too, has passed away. His words also live on. Even Danny Setter has passed on.

On the occasions when I'd run into Jerry Kramer, Jim Taylor, Forrest Gregg, Herb Adderley, Ray Nitschke, and Dave Robinson over the years, either in Canton or Green Bay, I'd ask about their memories of the Chiefs and that first AFL-NFL championship game, which provided me the Packer perspective.

This is a story about how an owner, players, coaches, and a fan base that were embarrassed in the first-ever game played between the AFL and NFL resurrected themselves to become and follow the best team in professional football three short years later. The team that history forgot in 1966 became a team to remember in 1969.

All these years later, those losses to the Chiefs at Trombly no longer sting.

The AFL 1

Lamar Hunt's childhood nickname was "Games."

He played them. He loved them. He lived for his games. Hunt had a special passion for sporting games. This was a man who honeymooned with his wife Norma at the 1964 Winter Olympic Games in Innsbruck, Austria. A man who founded Major League Soccer (MLS) and World Championship Tennis (WCT). A man who was an original investor in the National Basketball Association (NBA) Chicago Bulls in 1966.

But his roots were in football. Hunt walked onto the Southern Methodist University (SMU) football team in 1953 and spent three years with the Mustangs, all as a reserve offensive end. Hunt didn't catch many passes. No one did back then—not even the guy ahead of Hunt on the SMU depth chart, Raymond Berry. Decades later Berry was voted to the National Football League's (NFL) Centennial Team in 2019 as one of the one hundred greatest players in pro football history and one of its ten best pass catchers. But there was no indication of what was to come at SMU, where Berry caught just thirty-three passes in three seasons. The game of football was played on the ground then, not in the air.

Berry left SMU for the NFL in 1954, becoming a 20th-round draft pick of the Baltimore Colts. Another of Hunt's college teammates, Forrest Gregg, also was voted to the NFL Centennial Team as one of the game's one hundred greatest players and one of its seven best offensive tackles. He left SMU in 1956 for the Green Bay Packers, who drafted him with a second-round pick.

Their departures were a continuation of a trend that struck a nerve with Hunt. Texas was a large, fertile, and proud football state. Davey O'Brien, Doak Walker, and John David Crow all won the Heisman Trophy at Texas colleges. But O'Brien left the state to play professional football in Philadelphia, and Walker left to continue his career in Detroit, as did Crow in Chicago.

All-Americans and Texas legends Sammy Baugh, Bobby Layne, and Kyle Rote also departed Texas to continue their football careers. Baugh went to Washington to play for the Redskins, Layne went to Chicago to play for the Bears, and Rote went to New York to play for the Giants. Rote was the first overall selection of an NFL draft, Layne was a third overall choice in his, and Baugh went sixth overall.

Like oil, football talent gushed in Texas. Ki Aldrich of Texas Christian University (TCU) was the first overall pick of another NFL draft, Baylor quarterback Adrian Burk was a second overall choice, Walker went third overall, fellow SMU halfback Paul Page went fourth overall, and Baylor quarterbacks Cotton Davidson went fifth overall and Larry Isbell seventh.

Hunt pondered why all the great amateur players in his state had to leave Texas and travel to the northeastern quadrant of the country to continue their football careers. Baltimore, Chicago, Cleveland, Detroit, Green Bay, New York City, Philadelphia, Pittsburgh, and Washington DC were the faraway beneficiaries of the abundance of Texas talent. Not that Hunt had any aspirations of playing professionally himself—he would earn his SMU degree in geology with a position in the family oil business awaiting him upon graduation.

But "Games" kept the football exodus from his state on the back burner in his mind. He believed the passion for football in Texas could match any such passion in New York, Ohio, or Pennsylvania. College football games in Austin and Dallas were drawing crowds of sixty-thousand-plus every Saturday—easily topping the twenty and thirty thousand that were showing up in NFL stadiums on Sunday afternoons.

"When I was growing up, I participated in football but was always interested in the business side of it—the number of people who attended games," Hunt said. "That was the first thing I read in the baseball box scores. In the late 1940s, I was sixteen or seventeen and remember Doak Walker becoming a big name at SMU and the crowds they drew. That business side really attracted me. Dallas had become sort of a mecca for college football in the South. After I got out of SMU, I thought it could be a successful venture in Dallas, so I pursued it from that end."

So, at twenty-six years of age, Hunt set out to buy an NFL franchise that he could bring to Dallas. Calls to the NFL office in Philadelphia pointed him in the direction of Chicago, where there were two football teams, the Bears and Cardinals. George Halas owned and operated the Bears, the NFL's flagship franchise, and they weren't leaving Chicago. So the target became the Cardinals, who were owned by Violet (Bidwill) Wolfner and her family.

"I talked to the NFL in both 1958 and 1959 about expansion, and each time they directed me to the Wolfners," Hunt said. "But the Wolfners were not interested in moving the team. So at that point I thought, 'Hey, how about a new league? Why wouldn't the American and National in football make as much sense as the American and National in baseball?'"

His first call went downstate to fellow oilman Bud Adams in Houston.

"The game had been centered in the northern and eastern parts of the country, except for the 49ers and the Rams," Hunt said. "The other ten teams were all up in the Northeast. The whole basis of the American Football League (AFL) plan was to have teams in Dallas and Houston as rivals, much like the NFL had the Rams and 49ers in California. A rivalry with Houston, I thought, was a natural."

Texas wasn't the only market with a hunger for professional football. The AFL would open the door to virgin markets in Boston, Buffalo, Denver, and Minneapolis as well. The AFL needed a presence in major markets to attract a national television contract, so teams were also placed in New York City, Los Angeles, and the Bay Area.

And the "Foolish Club" was born—made up of the owners of the eight original franchises: Barron Hilton, Ralph Wilson, Harry Wismer, Bud Adams, Bob Howsam, Billy Sullivan, Max Winter, and Lamar Hunt. They needed deep pockets to challenge a league the stature of the NFL with four decades of history already in the books—and the AFL wore those deep pockets. And those pockets were enriched by the league's unique television contract with ABC, which gave all teams, big market and small, an equal share of the revenue—the first such TV sharing deal by any American sports league.

"We were awfully lucky in the people we attracted to the ownership aspect," Hunt explained. "They were people really interested in staying with it. Even after some twenty years, we still had six of the eight original ownership groups represented."

The new league got the attention of the NFL before a single football was ever passed or punted. The NFL stole the Minneapolis market and the Winter ownership group away from the AFL, promising an expansion franchise for the 1961 season. The NFL also went after the two biggest fish in the AFL pond.

"The NFL wanted the Dallas and Houston markets and offered Bud and myself the opportunity to come in and take the franchises," Hunt said. "But we really couldn't do that, nor did we want to do that because I had actively sought to commit people to a new league. I wasn't in a position to desert them."

And the war was on. The NFL was the established league with the credibility. The AFL was the upstart league with the money. The AFL signed the first, third, sixth, and 10th overall picks of the 1960 NFL draft. Hunt's Dallas Texans claimed two of them, signing third overall choice Johnny Robinson of Louisiana State University (LSU) away from the Detroit Lions and sixth overall choice Jack Spikes of TCU away from the Pittsburgh Steelers.

But the biggest blow was delivered by Adams. The Los Angeles Rams drafted Heisman Trophy winner Billy Cannon of LSU with the first overall selection of the 1960 draft. But Adams lured him instead to the Houston Oilers. The Los Angeles Chargers also scored in the spending war, signing Southern Cal offensive tackle Ron Mix away from the Baltimore Colts, who drafted him with the 10th overall choice of that draft.

The AFL signed veteran NFL quarterbacks George Blanda, Cotton Davidson, Jack Kemp, Babe Parilli, and Frank Tripucka, providing some recognizable names at the sport's key position. The AFL landed another recognizable name—Sid Gillman—as general manager and head coach of the Chargers. He coached the Los Angeles Rams for five seasons, taking them to one NFL title game, but was fired after a 2–10 finish in 1959. So Gillman moved across town to coach the Chargers in 1960.

With teams in Dallas, Denver, Houston, Los Angeles, and Oakland, the AFL was expanding pro football's horizons, pushing the sport deep into the South and well west of the Mississippi.

"Looking back, the timing was very right for there to be a second league," Hunt said. "The AFL helped popularize the game on a national basis. We took football into a lot of new areas. The AFL made it a national game and nurtured the rivalry that eventually led to the Super Bowl."

After Hunt turned down the NFL and the chance to own a franchise in the league he long wanted to join, the NFL declared war on Hunt. The NFL awarded an expansion franchise in Dallas to Clint Murchison in 1960. The Cowboys and Texans would share the same stadium and compete for the same entertainment dollar.

The war was indeed on.

2 The Dallas Texans

The city of Dallas actually had professional football before Lamar Hunt waded into ownership.

Briefly.

The Boston Yanks of 1948 became the New York Bulldogs in 1949 and then the New York Yanks in 1950 before finally moving to Dallas in 1952 to become the Texans. The vagabond franchise was terrible, finishing 3–9 in Boston in 1948, 1-9-2 in New York in 1951, and 1–11 in Dallas in 1952.

The Texans struggled on the field and off, failing to pay their bills. So the NFL reclaimed the franchise that November, and the Texans finished out the season playing on the road with their lone "home" game in Akron, Ohio. At year's end, the NFL awarded Carroll Rosenbloom an expansion franchise for Baltimore, and he purchased the roster and assets of the Texans, including future Hall of Fame defensive end Gino Marchetti.

The death of one football franchise spawned the birth of another.

"We chose the name 'Texans' because there had been an NFL team that lasted half a season here," Hunt explained. "It left very much of a black mark on Dallas and pro football as a site. There was a feeling that the colleges were just too strong. In my perverse line of thinking, I wanted that name to correct the bad image. It was a name associated with professional football. I liked the idea of the state of Texas on the helmet with the little star for Dallas."

But there would be more Texas flavor than just the logo on the side of the helmet. Hunt planned to build his Texas team with Texas players—for two obvious reasons. First, Hunt was partial to the talent his state was producing. Second, the players in uniform would be recognizable as the Texans attempted to convert the hardcore college football fans of the state into professional football fans.

"The first two to three years we probably had 50 percent of our roster from Texas," said linebacker Sherrill Headrick, who signed with the Texans as an undrafted free agent from TCU in 1960 and earned first-team All-Pro as a rookie.

In the league's very first draft, each of the eight franchises was awarded one "territorial" pick. The Texans used theirs on SMU's consensus All-American quarterback Don Meredith. The AFL then staged a 53-round draft over two days for the initial stocking of rosters. The Minneapolis franchise participated, but when Max Winter bolted for the NFL, the AFL awarded Oakland the eighth franchise and gave the Raiders the players drafted by Minneapolis.

Hunt loaded up. The Texans took tackle Gary Ferguson from SMU, safety Austin "Goose" Gonsoulin from Baylor, and the North Texas State backfield tandem of quarterback Vernon Cole and halfback Abner Haynes. Dallas also drafted TCU center Arvie Martin, Rice halfback Gordon Speer, and signed a couple of veteran free agents who had been previous NFL draft picks: offensive tackle Jerry Cornelison of SMU and halfback Jim Swink of TCU.

"It really felt like a Texas team and a Southwest Conference team," Cornelison said. "We felt we were going to be a Texas dynasty."

But Gonsoulin wouldn't be a part of that dynasty. His career as a Texan lasted barely a month. He was traded after the AFL draft to the Denver Broncos for the rights to fullback Jack Spikes of TCU.

"I wanted to play for the Texans so bad," said Gonsoulin, who would be named to the AFL's All-Time Team at decade's end. "I knew Johnny Robinson and some of the guys. I played in the College All-Star Game, but they traded me before we ever played. So I always thought the Texans were halfway my team."

There was another trade for Spikes in the works. A number of the college stars that year had signed contracts with both leagues, including LSU standouts Billy Cannon and Johnny Robinson, which needed to be sorted out by lawyers in the courts. The NFL Dallas Cowboys saw the same value in Spikes that the Texans did—he was local (TCU) and prominent, having earned consensus All-American honors with the Horned Frogs.

"The Cowboys called and told me they were going to make a trade with Pittsburgh and that they wanted me to be a Dallas Cowboy," Spikes said. "I told them I'd already signed my contract with Mr. Hunt. They said everybody's signing double contracts. I said, 'Not me. I've already told him I'm going to play for him, and that's what I'm going to do.'"

But the Texans lost out on their other All-American, Meredith, who signed with the Cowboys. So the Texans filled the void at the position by signing veteran free agent quarterback Cotton Davidson, who had been a first-round draft pick by the Baltimore Colts in 1954.

Signing Chris Burford was another coup for the Texans. He led the National Collegiate Athletic Association (NCAA) in receiving at Stanford in 1959 and was drafted by the NFL Cleveland Browns in addition to the Texans.

"I had some friends who played for the Browns," Burford said. "But the first couple weeks after the draft I never even heard from Cleveland. I said, the hell with them. When they did call, I told them I already made an appointment to meet with the owner of this Dallas team. But they didn't want me to talk to Lamar. I said, 'No, they're coming out here, and I'm going to talk to them. I never did go to Cleveland and never really talked to anyone there any further. They had the attitude back in those days they thought they were high and mighty. And, of course, in those days they were. There was no competition for them."

But now there was competition. It would be more of the same stocking philosophy for the Texans in 1961 when Dallas took Texas Tech linebacker E. J. Holub with its first-round selection, TCU defensive tackle Bob Lilly with its second choice, and SMU defensive end Jerry Mays in the fifth round. The Texans also drafted two of Mays's SMU teammates: halfback Glynn Gregory in the 13th round and wide receiver Frank Jackson in the 19th.

Holub, a consensus All-American, was a huge get for the Texans—offset by the loss of Lilly, another consensus All-American who opted to join Meredith with the rival Cowboys.

Just as Hunt was familiar with the players he was plucking off of Texas college campuses, he was familiar with the man he hired to become the first head coach of the Texans: Hank Stram, who spent a season as an assistant coach at SMU in 1956. Stram then spent two years at Notre Dame and another at the University of Miami before Hunt came calling with his offer to coach the Texans.

Stram's background was on the offensive side of the ball. Hunt knew that offensive football was entertaining—and the AFL would need to entertain right out of the gate. So Stram and his merry band of Texans gathered that summer for the franchise's inaugural training camp in Roswell, New Mexico. Players from the major college programs such as Robinson and Burford found that their new professional facilities were a step down from their days on campus.

"That place was unbelievable," said Burford. "We'd have been better off on a flying saucer. We stayed at the New Mexico Military Institute. It was hotter than hell, and there was no air conditioning because they didn't have summer school there. There were no screens on the windows, and there were mosquitos the size of B-25s flying around. They used to have these big irrigation ditches that ran around the fields for pumping water. After practice we'd just run over and flop in those ditches. It was a different world back then."

Stram was a little man with a big swagger. He was less concerned with Roswell than he was with Boston, Buffalo, Houston, and Oakland. He had a belief in himself, and he needed his players along for the ride.

"We sold them from the very first day, from the very first meeting, at our very first training camp," Stram said. "I told them, 'Before we even start this meeting I'm going to tell you one thing—I don't know how long we're going to be a team in the American Football League. It might be five years, four years, three years, or ten years. I don't know. No one does. But I guarantee one thing: when it's over, we're going to be the winningest team in the history of this league.'"

Stram was selling success—and he found a group of players willing to buy into his sales pitch.

"I don't think you can be a leader of men unless you do a great job of selling," Stram explained. "And if you don't believe what you're selling, you're never going to win."

There were nervous moments throughout camp for this collection of castoffs and youngsters. There were no incumbent starters—just twenty-two starting jobs to win and thirty-three roster spots to claim. The ultimate goal was to represent the Texans on the field in the fall. The immediate goal, however, was survival.

Stram conducted two practices per day—"full pads, full contact, full hitting," according to Cornelison.

"It was exhausting," he said. "In those days they wouldn't let you drink water during practice. So the ball boys would soak towels in buckets of water, then pass around the towels for the guys to suck on. You might be the third or fourth guy to suck on the same towel. Training camp was a real travesty. I don't know how we made it. I know there were a lot of people who didn't show up for practice after the first three to four days. They just got in a car and went home."

Hunt had his favorites and so did Stram. He coached linebacker Walt Corey in Miami in 1959. The AFL and NFL combined to make 680 draft choices in 1960, and Corey wasn't one of them. He was undersized for his position at 185 pounds, but his style of play was contagious. So Stram offered him a free agent contract.

"Hank knew I was going to hit people," Corey said.

But it didn't appear Corey would get that chance in the AFL. There were twenty linebackers in the Dallas training camp, and by the fourth exhibition game against the New York Titans in Abilene, Texas, Corey was invisible.

"I was on the cut list," Corey said. "My position coach said I was slower than any of the linebackers, so it came down to me and another guy. Hank called me in and told me, 'We're going to keep so-and-so because he's faster than you.' At that time, I had strained ligaments in my knee and was playing with it all bandaged up. So I said, 'Hank, I don't mind getting waived, but you're cutting me for the wrong reasons. You're cutting me because I'm the slowest, and that's not right. I'm the fastest. Even with my bad knee I can beat that guy by 5 yards in a 40-yard dash.'

"So we're playing our next exhibition game in Little Rock, and Hank says, 'I'll tell you what I'll do. When we get to Little Rock, we'll run some 40-yard dashes.' We ran them. I did win them by over 5 yards, and he cut the other guy that night."

Corey started for the Texans that season.

There was one certainty for Stram in training camp—the Texans would be able to run the football. Dallas could line up three backs behind Davidson that the NFL coveted: Robinson, Spikes, and Abner Haynes. Robinson and Spikes were both selected in the top six picks of the 1960 NFL draft, and Haynes was a fifth-round choice of the Pittsburgh Steelers.

Also with the Texans in camp was Jim Swink, the Heisman Trophy runner-up in 1955, after rushing for 1,283 yards and leading the NCAA in scoring with 125 points. He became a second-round draft pick of the Chicago Bears in 1957 but elected to attend medical school rather than play professional football. Three years later, when the AFL arrived and offered Swink the chance to pursue a football career closer to home, he signed with the Texans.

Stram saw elements of his team that he liked in training camp that summer. He found a lot more to like in August.

Dallas

3

Football was not the year-round venture for NFL players in the 1960s that it is today.

There were no offseason programs then, no minicamps, no quarterback schools. Players went to training camp in July, and the season officially ended in late December with the NFL championship game. That left six months—half of the year—for players to supplement their modest football incomes with offseason employment. You weren't going to get rich playing offensive line or linebacker in the NFL. So some players spent their offseason as teachers. Some were salesmen. Some ran gas stations, drove delivery trucks, or worked construction.

Staying in football shape twelve months out of the year wasn't the focus of the players back then. Making car payments, house payments, and putting food on the table was. Training camp was when and where players got their minds and bodies back into football mode.

In those days pro football teams spent more than two months in camp. The players would use the first two to three weeks getting into shape physically as the coaches installed the offensive and defensive systems. Then each team would play six exhibition games to give the coaches an idea of who could play, who couldn't, and who would still be around come September.

And back then, teams played the exhibition games to win. Vince Lombardi won 73.9 percent of his games in his ten-year, Hall of Fame head coaching career, the third-best in NFL history. He was even better when the games didn't matter, winning 78.5 percent of the exhibition games during those ten seasons. Winning mattered to Lombardi—and it mattered to the NFL. Winning was habit-forming. So was losing.

No team was sitting out its entire starting lineup in the preseason as the Los Angeles Rams did in 2021 on the way to winning a Super Bowl. Starters often would play deep into the fourth quarter in those August games of the 1960s, readying their bodies for the full-speed contact that awaited them in the fall.

Exhibition games were not part of a team's season ticket package back then. Even though the August tickets were less expensive, the games didn't count, so there was no rush in local markets to buy them up. Because of that, teams favored taking the exhibition show on the road. The Cowboys and Texans both played six preseason games in 1960 but only one apiece at the Cotton Bowl. The other five games were scattered across the country. The Cowboys played games in Bloomington, Minnesota, Pendleton, Oregon, Louisville, San Antonio, and Seattle. The Texans played games in Abilene, Little Rock, and Tulsa.

The Cowboys had a roster of young players as well as older—NFL castoffs acquired in the expansion draft. This group was not ready for prime time. The Cowboys lost their first two exhibition games to San Francisco and St. Louis before returning to Dallas for their one home date against Johnny Unitas and the Baltimore Colts. A crowd of forty thousand showed up to see the return of professional football to Dallas. That crowd also saw the Cowboys lose their third straight game, 14–10.

The Cowboys managed to win only one of their six preseason games to stagger into September and the regular season. But there was no such stagger for the rival Texans, who saved their one home exhibition game for the preseason finale. The Texans brought a 5–0 record home to the Cotton Bowl to play their natural rival, the Houston Oilers.

A crowd of 51,000 turned out to see a team with AFL championship aspirations. It was the largest home crowd either Dallas team saw in their first three seasons, regular or exhibition. The Texans treated that huge crowd to a 24–3 victory for a perfect exhibition schedule.

"Winning was everything with Hank (Stram)," offensive tackle Jerry Cornelison said. "It was a pride thing. He was trying to show off that he was a head coach, that he knew what he was doing—that he could turn this bunch of ragamuffins into a football team. Which he did."

But the Texans were realistic. As were the Cowboys. The fifty-one thousand that cheered the Texans that night were still twenty-four thousand bodies shy of a sellout. Neither the Cowboys nor the Texans had the marquee value of SMU. So it would have been folly for the Cowboys or the Texans, a pair of start-up franchises, to expect any sellouts in 1960. The goal was to get as many keisters in the seats on Sundays with the hopes of building a following.

"The Cowboys established their prices in 1960 at $3.90 for a reserved seat," Lamar Hunt said. "That's exactly what the colleges charged. But we pulled a coup on them. We went ten cents higher. We charged four dollars, and our rationale was this is professional football and we're better than colleges. It was that kind of war of nerves constantly. Certainly ten cents was not going to make or break our ticket sales. But there were little things like that every day."

The Texans lost the season opener in Los Angeles to the Chargers, and Stram had to wait until the second weekend for his first head-coaching victory. Cowboys coach Tom Landry had to wait until the 1961 season opener for his first victory. The Texans finished the 1960 regular season 8–6 for second place in the Western Division behind the Chargers. The Cowboys finished 0-11-1 for last place in the Eastern Division.

The scheduling was easy that first season.

"The AFL moved to Dallas before the NFL, so the Texans were given the first choice of dates," Hunt said.

Not that the home field mattered much. The big crowds of August became a distant memory. The Texans averaged only 24,500 fans per game that inaugural season, the Cowboys just 21,471. Only ten thousand showed up to see the Cowboys' home finale against the San Francisco 49ers.

"The public saw fourteen games for free on television," Hunt explained. "They would see seven Cowboys' games on the road and seven Texans' games on the road. So they never went to games. Why ever go to a game when you can see one every Sunday? It was painful financially and disappointing to see the crowds out there. It was hard to live through."

The Texans took a step backward in 1961, finishing 6–8, while the Cowboys took a step forward, finishing 4-9-1. But worse for Hunt, the city and team he wanted in his new league to serve as the natural rival for his Texans—the Houston Oilers—won each of the first two AFL championships. And even worse for the Texans, the Cowboys won at the gate in

1961. The Cowboys averaged 24,571 fans per game, the Texans a modest 17,571. Only eight thousand showed up in December to see the Texans host the Denver Broncos.

And the bickering heightened between the two franchises.

"You reveled when the other side had a bad crowd, and they did the same to us," Hunt said. "They would ridicule the fact that we had inflated our gates . . . and we ridiculed the fact the Cowboys let in kids for free. One paid adult and four kids could get in free."

The Texans were developing stars, and the Cowboys weren't. Haynes was the AFL MVP in 1960 and league rushing champion. He joined Cotton Davidson, Chris Burford, Sherrill Headrick, E. J. Holub, and five other teammates as AFL All-Stars in 1961. The Cowboys produced only two NFL All-Stars in 1961: running back Don Perkins and journeyman tight end Dick Bielski.

There was no major league baseball, basketball, or hockey in Dallas in 1960, so the choice beat at the city's newspapers was pro football. The competition was as fierce among the beat reporters off the field as it was between the two teams on the field.

"The news coverage was unbelievable," Hunt said. "And I thought, frankly, that they were very fair. I understand it used to infuriate Tex (Hall of Fame president Schramm) and the Cowboys that they would give this new league equal billing. But the newspapers wanted to be fair to both—and we happened to have a better record.

"The crowning blow came after the 1961 season when the [Dallas] Times Herald named an All-Dallas All-Pro team—a twenty-four-position team, the best eleven offensive players, the best eleven defensive players, and the specialists. They had it virtually down the line with an even split between the Texans and Cowboys. I understand that rankled the Cowboys. They were trying to sell that they were the better product."

The Cowboys certainly weren't the better product in 1962. Two additions by the Texans, one on offense and one on defense, would dramatically change the fortunes of the franchise. Stram dug deep into his memory back for Len Dawson and Johnny Robinson.

And suddenly the Texans were a juggernaut.

Len Dawson 4

Len Dawson knew he was special long before any adult could identify such traits in him.

Mel Knowlton was the football coach at Alliance (Ohio) High School and was closing the 1950 season with his once-in-a-lifetime quarterback. John Borton was an all-state selection for Alliance and was soon heading off to Ohio State on a football scholarship.

As Knowlton was sitting in his coaching office following the season finale, he turned to his assistant coaches and asked, "Well, who's going to replace Borton?"

The school's fourth-string quarterback—a scrawny five-eight, 130-pound sophomore—overheard the conversation and piped in, "I'm the guy, coach. It's going to be me."

Knowlton smiled and could only shake his head. Little Lenny Dawson had given no indication that fall that he could ever be a starter on the Alliance team—much less *the* starter at the most important position on the field.

"I was a bag man," Dawson said of his sophomore season. "I was one of the guys holding the dummies at practice. I got the stuffing knocked out of me. There was a first team, a second team, a third team, a fourth team, and 'the rest of you guys.' I was one of 'the rest of you's.' We had an offensive line that averaged about two hundred pounds, and I hadn't started to develop physically yet. I was little. I used to literally hide behind the goalposts hoping he (Knowlton) wouldn't see me."

Knowlton doubled as coach of the varsity basketball team and was surprised to see Dawson win a starting spot that winter on his senior-laden team. A growth spurt arrived, and Dawson added four inches and twenty pounds by spring practice. He started the offseason as the third-string quarterback but finished as the starter.

"Len told me he was going to be better than Borton," Knowlton said. "He told me he was going to be the best."

That would be a tall order. Borton left Alliance to become a starting quarterback at Ohio State, throwing a school record of five touchdown passes in a 1952 game for the Buckeyes. That mark stood for forty-two years. He threw for a school record with 312 yards in another game. That mark stayed on the books for twenty-nine years. Borton became a co-captain of the Buckeyes as a senior in 1954 and went on to play a season in the NFL with the Cleveland Browns.

But Knowlton started to believe in Dawson when Alliance took its longest road trip of the 1951 season—250 miles for a game at Middleton, Ohio.

"Taking a bunch of high school kids on a five-hour bus ride and then playing a game that night is not an easy thing to do," Knowlton said. "It was cold, and we had our first snowfall that night. We got beat, 32–21, but Lenny threw three touchdown passes. He was the only guy in the stadium the weather didn't affect. The Middleton coaches marveled at him. They couldn't believe that any young high school kid could handle the ball like he did and throw like he did in that weather. He was as good in bad weather as he was in good weather."

In two years as a starter, Dawson set school-passing records with his 3,107 yards and twenty-six touchdowns. He also became the only player in Alliance history named all-state in both football and basketball in the same academic school year.

"Ohio State wanted Len so bad they could taste it," Knowlton said. "But he wouldn't have fit at Ohio State like he did at Purdue. Purdue was a passing team. Woody (Hayes) was molding most of his Ohio State teams into power teams. And John (Borton) was already at Ohio State. Len told me, 'There's no sense going down there and battling with Borton. I might as well go someplace he ain't.'"

Borton wasn't at Purdue. But Hank Stram was. He was the assistant coach charged with recruiting the Alliance wunderkind.

"Purdue played a style of football that utilized his abilities," Knowlton said.

Indeed. The NCAA did not allow freshmen to play football until 1972, so Dawson didn't hit the field until his sophomore season in 1954. But he arrived with a thunderclap.

"We opened the season against Missouri," Stram explained, "so I said to him, 'Good luck in your first collegiate game for Purdue University.' He said, 'Thank you, coach, but you don't need luck. You need ability.' Then he proceeded to throw four touchdown passes and lead us to a 31–0 victory over Missouri. Then he threw four more touchdown passes in a 27–14 road victory at Notre Dame."

Notre Dame entered the game ranked No. 1 in the country. That put Dawson on the college football map—and he stayed there for the next three seasons. Just as he did at Alliance, Dawson left Purdue with the school records for passing yards (3,325) and touchdowns (twenty-nine).

Dawson became the fifth overall selection of the 1957 NFL draft, going to the Pittsburgh Steelers one choice ahead of Jim Brown. But Dawson sat behind Earl Morrall and Jack Kemp in his rookie season. His chance of seeing the field dimmed considerably in 1958 when coach Buddy Parker traded for Bobby Layne, forging a reunion of a coach-quarterback combination that produced a pair of NFL titles earlier that decade for the Detroit Lions.

Dawson threw only seventeen passes in his three seasons with the Steelers before he was traded to the Browns in 1960. He threw only twenty-eight more passes in two years there as he sat behind Milt Plum. His NFL career was bottoming out so he asked Browns coach Paul Brown for his release.

And that's when he got yet another recruiting call from Stram—a familiar face offering up a new league, a new opportunity.

"To tell you the truth, I was awful after five years of not playing in the NFL," Dawson said. "The skills that I once had eroded. Had it not been for Hank Stram, there would not have been a second look for the seventh son of a seventh son. He stayed with me. He felt there was still something there. He was my saving grace."

Still, the move was puzzling. The Texans already had Cotton Davidson, who was the MVP of the 1961 AFL All-Star Game. Wide receiver Chris Burford had developed a rapport with Davidson, catching fifty-one passes from him in 1961 to lead the Texans and join his quarterback at the All-Star Game.

"When Lenny first came to us he had a cracker arm," Burford said. "He hadn't played for so long that his arm was really weak. Cotton was an older guy and good quarterback with a really strong arm. He had velocity and could really put something on the ball. Lenny was more of a placement quarterback. When he first came, the jury was out. His arm was so weak."

But the more Dawson threw in training camp, the stronger his arm became.

"We signed Len in the summer of 1962," Lamar Hunt said. "He came to training camp and was terrible. But as the preseason games went on, he got to play a little more and a little more. Finally, by the last preseason game, he was our starting quarterback and had quite a good game against the Patriots in the Cotton Bowl. He was terrific. In two months after reuniting with Stram, he had gotten in shape and gotten his mechanics back."

Stram had a comfort level with Dawson. But he also had a comfort level with Davidson, who doubled as the team's punter. That's when Hunt stepped in.

"With a thirty-three-man roster, I can't remember where the idea originated or who made the initial contact, but the Raiders had an interest in Cotton Davidson," Hunt said. "He was not going to play for us at that point. The Raiders had a bad team, so I figured we could get a high draft choice from them. So I asked them for a No. 1 draft pick. It sounded good to me. I didn't talk to Hank about it—and he almost quit over it. He was looking at it in the short term. What if Dawson got hurt? Then he'd be playing with a rookie (Eddie Wilson). Fortunately, that didn't happen."

Dallas won its first three games that season and six of the first seven with Dawson at the helm. The Texans were warming to their new quarterback.

"Len had a fabulous knack of putting the ball in the right spots," Burford said. "It didn't have any velocity on it, but it didn't need any. It got to me at the right time. Very accurate. More accurate than Cotton by far. As time went on he got stronger and stronger. He got more into the offense, and he had that great touch on his passes."

Dawson quarterbacked the Texans to an 11–3 record and a Western Division championship. He won the AFL passing title that year, completing a league-best 61 percent of his throws with a league-best twenty-nine touchdown passes. His play helped Dallas earn a spot in the AFL championship game at Houston where the Texans faced the daunting task of unseating the two-time champion Oilers.

"Len Dawson was the all-time luckiest thing that ever happened to the Chiefs," Hunt said. "I didn't expect much because I didn't believe you could turn a player loose with that kind of ability. It was amazing a guy could go five years without playing, then turn it on as soon as he got a chance."

Even though Houston was a touchdown favorite, Dallas prevailed 20–17 in double overtime on a Tommy Brooker field goal. Dawson threw only fourteen passes but completed nine of them for 88 yards and a touchdown as the Texans relied on their ball-control rushing attack to keep George Blanda and the mighty Houston offense off the field. The Texans ran the ball fifty-four times, and Dawson didn't commit any turnovers. Blanda did, throwing five interceptions.

And the city of Dallas had its first pro football champion.

"His acquisition was really the turning point of our franchise," said Stram of his quarterback.

Over on defense, there was another turning point.

Johnny Robinson

5

Johnny Robinson couldn't escape the long shadow of fellow halfback Billy Cannon at LSU.

LSU finished as the only unbeaten, untied team in the nation in 1958 on the way to the first national title in school history. Robinson was selected first-team All-SEC (Southeastern Conference) on the strength of his 480 rushing yards and five touchdowns. But Cannon was selected first-team All-America. Robinson was an All-SEC selection again in 1959, but Cannon won the Heisman Trophy as college football's best player.

When the NFL sat down for the 1960 college draft, the Detroit Lions selected Robinson with the third overall selection. But the Los Angeles Rams claimed Cannon with the first overall choice.

Robinson finally found a place to share the spotlight with Cannon—in court. The two players agreed contractually to play football with both the AFL and NFL, Cannon with the Houston Oilers and Robinson with the Dallas Texans. The four teams involved would need lawyers and judges to sort the mess out.

The NFL was going to face competition from a new league for the first time ever in 1960 and was anxious to lock down the college game's biggest names and best players. The only chance the AFL would have against the NFL was to plaster some recognizable names on its marquee. But the NFL moved swiftly to prevent that, starting on the LSU campus in December where Cannon and Robinson were preparing for the Sugar Bowl against Mississippi.

"I always wanted to play in the NFL," Robinson said. "There was more competition over there. I hadn't even heard from Dallas. So I met a (NFL) scout in the hotel in Baton Rouge. I still had eligibility left and signed then."

The two AFL teams then swooped in after LSU lost to Ole Miss. Immediately after the game, in fact.

"I signed my contract with Dallas underneath the goalpost at the Sugar Bowl," Robinson recalled.

But Robinson was more cautious with his AFL contract than his NFL contract. He signed with the Lions to play football. But he didn't sign a football contract with the AFL. Theo Cangelosi, a member of the board of supervisors at LSU who was advising Robinson, devised a creative alternative in the contract negotiations with the Texans.

"He suggested we negotiate a contract with (Hunt-owned) Penrod Oil just in case they (the AFL) didn't make it," Robinson said. "It was a three-year personal services contract with Lamar. I worked for the company."

Along the way, Robinson began suffering buyer's remorse over his signing with the Lions.

"To be honest with you, I was a little bit afraid of going up there (to Detroit) and playing in the snow," Robinson said. "Playing in the cold in Detroit didn't really appeal to me. Given a choice, I'd rather be in Dallas. It was closer to home."

Robinson was the one person in the courts who couldn't lose. Even if the Lions were declared the rightful owner of his football contract, Robinson would still have a personal services contract in place with Hunt. But it didn't come to that.

"Lamar's attorneys got involved and got the (NFL) contract declared illegal because it was signed prior to the Sugar Bowl," Robinson said. "Billy did the same thing. It wasn't one of my proudest moments. If I had to do it over again, I wouldn't have signed the Detroit contract."

That gave the AFL two of the college game's biggest stars for its inaugural season. It also gave the Texans instant credibility on offense. Hank Stram's backfield of Johnny Robinson, Jack Spikes, and Abner Haynes could have started for most NFL teams in 1960.

And that trio delivered on the lofty expectations. Haynes rushed for 975 yards to lead the league and capture Most Valuable Player honors. Robinson added 458 yards and Spikes 457 as the Texans rushed for 2,007 yards and a league-best twenty-four touchdowns. But the Oilers led the league in passing and used the arm of George Blanda to win the inaugural AFL championship.

It was more of the same in 1961. Haynes again led the team in rushing with 841 yards. Spikes added 314 yards and Robinson 200 as the Texans collectively led the league in rushing. But the Oilers again led the league in passing, and this time Blanda was the AFL MVP. He threw for professional football record thirty-six touchdowns, and the Oilers repeated as league champions.

Robinson flashed the hands for the Texans that he didn't flash in college, having caught only thirty-four passes in his career at LSU. But he caught forty-one passes as a rookie and a team runnerup thirty-five more in 1961. He scored more touchdowns catching the ball (nine) in his first two AFL seasons than he did running it (six).

That got Stram to thinking—and dipping into his memory bank. Specifically, a 1958 game between Miami and LSU when Stram was on the Hurricanes' coaching staff and the SEC team crushed the Floridians, 41–0.

"I played both ways at LSU," Robinson said. "So did Billy."

Not only did Robinson play defensive back for the Tigers, he played it exceptionally well. LSU selected its All-Century football team in 1993 and named Cannon as one of the four running backs and Robinson as one of the four defensive backs. You don't need to be on offense to catch the football.

"Hank called me in and said we've got these two guys coming in (at running back in 1962) and I would like to move you to defense," Robinson said. "When we (LSU) played them (Miami) down there, he told me he always thought I was going to be a defensive back."

His ball skills were only part of the motivation for the position change. His athleticism also played a part. Robinson lettered in baseball at LSU and also won SEC singles and doubles championship in tennis. His quick hands, feet, and reactions were evident in whatever sport he played. There also was his style of play. He was a physical runner on offense and would take that physicality over to the defensive side of the ball.

"Johnny was a head hunter," said wide receiver Frank Jackson. "He was a hard hitter and so athletic—he could explode on people like a linebacker."

Hall of Fame wide receiver Lance Alworth of the Chargers added, "When we ran crossing patterns against Kansas City, I knew I was going to get hit hard. I had to prepare myself for Johnny both mentally and physically. Simply put, he's one of the greatest safeties I ever faced. In fact, I can't think of any in the fifty years since then that have been better."

With Robinson at free safety, the Texans engineered a defensive turnaround. They climbed from fifth in the AFL in defense in 1961 to first in 1962. They allowed the fewest points in the league—110 fewer than the previous season. The arrival of Dawson on offense allowed the Texans to vault from fourth in the AFL in offense in 1961 to first in 1962.

The Texans won the Western Division with an 11–3 record and then upset the Oilers in the AFL championship game. AFL MVP Blanda threw five interceptions, and Robinson was on the receiving end of two of them. Robinson also had four interceptions during the regular season.

Robinson finally escaped the shadow of Cannon, who caught six passes for the losing Oilers in that title game. And a Hall of Famer was born.

"I was used to playing defense and felt comfortable there," Robinson said. "Defense was the best move I ever made."

The Texans were putting the pieces in place for long-term success. But it wouldn't come in Dallas.

Kansas City 6

The offseason following the 1962 championship should have been an exhilarating one for Lamar Hunt and the Dallas Texans. Instead it was filled with disappointment for Hunt and frustration for his players.

The AFL Texans were a success on the field but not off it. The rival NFL Dallas Cowboys were not a success either on or off the field. Maybe Dallas wasn't the glowing professional football market that Hunt expected it to be.

In the three years since the inception of the franchise, the Texans posted an overall 25–17 record, never finishing lower than second in the Western Division and winning one championship. The Cowboys posted a 9-28-3 record, never finishing higher than fifth in the Eastern Conference.

The Texans outdrew the Cowboys in 1962, averaging crowds of 22,201 in the seventy-five-thousand-seat Cotton Bowl. The Cowboys drew an average of 21,784 for their games despite a far more attractive home schedule that featured games against Jim Brown and the Cleveland Browns, Y. A. Tittle and Sam Huff and the New York Giants, and John David Crow and the St. Louis Cardinals.

"There was a very intense rivalry between the two organizations," Hunt said. "But both of us were miserable failures at the gate. A lot of people don't realize how poorly both teams drew. We had a situation that our league was going to live or die only if its eight teams lived. We won the championship in 1962 and still averaged only about 10,100 paid. The Cowboys averaged about 9,900 paid. But they had a very poor record. The announced crowds were much smaller than they really were."

Despite having better players, a better team, and a far better record, the Texans were losing the battle at the gate in the three years they went head-to-head with the Cowboys. The NFL team averaged 22,649 for its twenty home games, and the AFL team averaged 21,424 for its twenty-one home games. The Cowboys drew only two crowds of forty-thousand-plus in three years—the Texans, just one.

Financially, Hunt had a decision to make. His timetable accelerated that January when Hunt received a telephone call from Kansas City Mayor H. Roe Bartle.

"Any interest in moving your team to Kansas City?" Bartle asked.

For three years Hunt's focus was making pro football work in Dallas. But the time had obviously come to shift his focus.

"The American Football League was a business venture, and the Texans were just a one-eighth part of it," Hunt explained. "If we were doing things to harm the venture's success . . . we needed to find a way to be successful. I couldn't sit there and butt my head against the wall when there was an opportunity to be elsewhere. We needed success stories—not martyrs who sit there and play before empty houses."

If there was interest from Kansas City, Hunt thought, might there be interest from other cities as well? There were certainly other towns starving for professional football. So Hunt began exploring his options. He took a long look at Atlanta and New Orleans in addition to Kansas City, and he heard from other cities too.

"Because my principal business interests were in Dallas, I wanted a place that would be relatively easy to get to," Hunt said. "So I wasn't interested in Miami or Seattle. I had been up to Kansas City for a baseball weekend series between the Yankees and the Athletics in 1958, and they sold out Municipal Stadium three straight games. That always impressed me.

"The stadium was certainly not the Cotton Bowl, but it was a good stadium. It also didn't have college football. After three years (in Dallas) I had learned that not having college football competition was probably an important factor. Oklahoma-Texas was drawing seventy-five thousand, SMU was drawing fifty to fifty-five thousand . . . and the poor Cowboys and Texans were drawing ten thousand."

So on February 8, 1963, Hunt announced the Texans were going to relocate to Kansas City. But there was one condition.

"We asked for a season ticket commitment," Hunt said. "We really asked for too much. We asked for twenty-five thousand, and they sold

15,182 . . . I can still remember the numbers. But that was so much higher than any team in the AFL. We also had the highest ticket prices. We went one dollar higher than the Chicago Bears. We charged six dollars for reserved seats and seven dollars for box seats."

That's where the frustration set in. The best team in the AFL had been run out of Dallas by one of the worst teams in the NFL.

"We offered to play the Cowboys loser-leave-town," Sherrill Headrick said, "and they chickened out. The game would have filled the stands for sure. But they didn't want to play us then. We had a better team than they did—a much better team—and we wanted to show them."

Hunt could feel the pain of his players.

"It was difficult because a large part of our team was from Texas—Jerry Mays, Abner Haynes, Jack Spikes, E. J. Holub . . . ," Hunt said. "We had an abnormal amount of Southwest Conference players. And guys like Fred Arbanas (Michigan State) and Jim Tyrer (Ohio State) adopted Dallas as their home and liked it very much. We were a championship team. But from a business standpoint, it was the only thing that made sense. Kansas City's civic ticket drive assured us that we'd be able to pay the bills."

The NFL had its small-market champion in Green Bay. Now the AFL had its small-market champion in Kansas City. It was a culture shock for both leagues.

"I loved Dallas," Chris Burford said. "I was attending law school at SMU, so I was into the community and expecting to stay there. I liked Texas. I liked Dallas. Sure we were disappointed. My wife and I just bought a house and lived in it for three months when they announced the team was moving.

"I was not happy. We felt we were winning the battle. We had just won the championships, but we never got the chance to bear any fruits from it. I'm sure Lamar was tired of losing money, and we probably became a more valuable franchise by moving to Kansas City. The Cowboys were losing money. Neither one of us was making any money."

Hunt agreed to move the team, but he was not prepared to leave the franchise's entire identity behind in Dallas.

"I wanted to keep the name (Texans)," Hunt said. "The Lakers stayed the Lakers when they went to California. Hank and I wanted to keep the name, but (club president) Jack Steadman convinced us that wasn't too smart and that it wouldn't sell. So we had a name-the-team contest, and we became the Chiefs."

The AFL was starting to turn the corner. The Chargers left Los Angeles after one apathetic season for San Diego, another football-hungry market, and now the Texans were heading to Kansas City. The AFL started sinking its roots into the football landscape.

"We found a new home for the Chargers; we found a new home for the Texans," Hunt said. "A new stadium was being built in New York for our team there; the Oilers had the Astrodome going up. We had other teams starting to draw—Houston, Denver . . . Once we had eight that could survive, we knew we would have a viable league."

The Chiefs didn't have the same success on the field the next three seasons in Kansas City that the Texans had the first three seasons in Dallas. But quietly, the Chiefs were building something special.

7 HBCU

Bill Nunn was enshrined in the Pro Football Hall of Fame in 2021 as a contributor.

Nunn was the sports editor of the national African American newspaper the *Pittsburgh Courier* in the 1950s and annually picked an All-American football team of players from historically Black colleges and universities (HBCU). He attended the games and watched the players with an eye for talent.

The Pittsburgh Steelers decided to tap into his expertise in 1967 when they hired Nunn as a part-time scout. He became full-time in 1969 when fellow Hall of Famer Chuck Noll became the head coach. Pittsburgh went on to win four Super Bowls in the 1970s.

Over the years Nunn would move talented HBCU players onto the Steelers' drafting radar—L. C. Greenwood (Arkansas AM&N, 1969), Mel Blount (Southern, 1970), Frank Lewis (Grambling State, 1971), Ernie Holmes (Texas Southern, 1971), Glen Edwards (Florida A&M, undrafted 1971), John Stallworth (Alabama A&M, 1974), and Donnie Shell (South Carolina State, undrafted 1974). All would start on Pittsburgh Super Bowl teams, and Blount, Stallworth, and Shell would wind up in the Pro Football Hall of Fame.

But there was another African American scout—the first such scout, in fact—doing what Nunn was doing except a decade earlier, finding HBCU players who could help his employer, the Kansas City Chiefs, become an AFL champion.

His name was Lloyd Wells, and, like Nunn, his background was in the media. He was a photographer living and working in Houston. As a Texas Southern graduate, he had a passion for sports and promoting young Black athletes. He was well-connected and later in life became a confidante of

Muhammad Ali. Lamar Hunt met Wells at a function at Texas Southern in the early 1960s and was impressed with his knowledge of HBCU players, who were invisible to most NFL teams at the time. So Hunt invited him to be part of the team's scouting think tank.

The Texans made history in 1963 when they used the first overall selection of the AFL draft, acquired from the Oakland Raiders in the Cotton Davidson deal, on Grambling defensive tackle Buck Buchanan.

A year before, running back Ernie Davis became the first African American selected No. 1 overall in an NFL draft by the Washington Redskins. But Davis was a known commodity. His legs carried Syracuse to a perfect 11–0 record and a national championship in 1959. He won the Heisman Trophy as college football's best player in 1961. There was game film of Davis performing against Notre Dame, Penn State, Texas, and UCLA—some of the top college teams in the nation—and dominating. He averaged 6.6 yards per carry in his career.

Buchanan was not a known commodity. His Grambling film featured games against Alcorn State, Benedict, Bishop, Prairie View A&M, Southern, and Wiley. Players from those teams were not clustered on any NFL draft boards. Buchanan was dominant—as well a man six-seven and 287 pounds should be against that level of competition.

The NFL didn't touch Buchanan until the 19th round with the 265th overall pick of its draft by the New York Giants. Buchanan started as a rookie for the Chiefs, collecting five sacks, and was voted to the AFL All-Star Game in his second season—the first of eight such postseason appearances.

"The biggest aspect was his physical size," Hunt said. "Ernie Ladd had come into the game one or two years earlier. He also was from Grambling and was an established AFL star. So it was looked upon as a wise choice then. Buck (Buchanan) was part of a pioneering effort."

Indeed. In 1964 the Chiefs started paying Wells for his thoughts, hiring him as the first African American scout in pro football, beating Nunn to the pay window by three years. And his sway in the Kansas City building was evident.

In 1964 the Chiefs signed undrafted college free agent Mack Lee Hill out of Southern. In 1965 the Chiefs drafted five players from the HBCU—

linemen Al Dotson and Frank Cornish, both of Grambling, and wide receivers Otis Taylor of Prairie View, Frank Pitts of Southern, and Gloster Richardson of Jackson State.

In 1966 the Chiefs drafted cornerback Fletcher Smith of Tennessee State and signed cornerback Emmitt Thomas of Bishop as an undrafted college free agent. Kansas City followed that up with linebacker Willie Lanier of Morgan State and return specialist Noland "Super Gnat" Smith of Tennessee State in 1967. Halfback Robert Holmes of Southern arrived in 1968, and cornerback Jim Marsalis of Tennessee State and tight end Morris Stroud of Clark Atlanta University in 1969.

Like Nunn, Wells put his stamp on three Hall of Famers—Buchanan, Lanier, and Thomas. Buchanan, Holmes, Lanier, Marsalis, Pitts, Taylor, and Thomas would all start in Super Bowls for the Chiefs. That's as many championship starters as Nunn supplied the Steelers.

More importantly, the work of Wells, Hunt, and the Chiefs opened football's door for Nunn and HBCU players. The Chiefs became colorblind—and the rest of pro football eventually followed suit.

"After first meeting Lamar in 1967 I came to know someone who was as balanced a man as I've ever met in terms of how he related to people," Lanier said. "He did not have a hierarchical structure. He dealt with everyone the same. Many of us weren't used to being around people like that. Lamar Hunt meant opportunity, equality of opportunity, and hope for a positive outcome, because coming out of school when I did, there were question marks about all of those things."

Big question marks. There were no African Americans in pro football at middle linebacker when Lanier came along. For decades, the NFL had been a closed fraternity of players and teams. But the arrival of the AFL created almost three hundred new employment openings for players. That put the best players from the HBCU in play. And the AFL was in a greater hurry to find them than the NFL.

"By forming the American Football League, Lamar created more job opportunities for the talent, regardless where it came from," Lanier said. "Eugene Upshaw came out at the same time (1967), when the only Black offensive lineman in the NFL was Jim Parker. When I came in there were no Black middle linebackers. If there's no American Football League, where would I have gone? Or Art Shell the next year? The jobs wouldn't have been there for us."

Wells was directly responsible for Otis Taylor's signing with the Chiefs. In 1965 the two leagues were engaged in a signing war, and during the draft they were busy stashing players—hiding them from the other league. Both the AFL and NFL were involved in the clandestine operation. A league would assign a team babysitter to a top draft prospect and check him into a hotel under an assumed name around the time of the draft. If the Chicago Bears were going to select a player, they wanted to make damn sure he was going to sign. The AFL couldn't sign a player if you couldn't find him, and vice versa.

Kansas City coveted Taylor but couldn't find him. But Wells had known Taylor since the player was in junior high school in Houston, and he plied family connections to pinpoint the motel in Taylor's hometown where the NFL was hiding him. In the middle of the night, Wells spirited Taylor out the window of his hotel room. A short time later they were on a flight to Kansas City where Taylor signed with the Chiefs.

Prairie View A&M became the first HBCU school ever invited to the National Association of Intercollegiate Athletics (NAIA) playoffs in 1963. Nunn proclaimed the Panthers the HBCU "national champion" in his *Pittsburgh Courier* in both 1963 and 1964, when they won nineteen of their twenty games with quarterback Jim Kearney throwing passes to Taylor.

The Detroit Lions selected Kearney in the 11th round of the 1965 NFL draft, but not as a quarterback. The perception then was that African Americans either weren't smart or talented enough to play the quarterback position in the NFL. It was a perception from the past that lingered well into the future. So the Lions projected Kearney as a defensive back, and he spent two seasons as a reserve in the NFL, suiting up for only thirteen of a possible twenty-eight games.

The Lions released Kearney in 1967, and he hopped aboard the HBCU train to Kansas City. He moved into the starting lineup at safety alongside Johnny Robinson and gave the Chiefs yet another HBCU product in the starting lineup of a Super Bowl.

The HBCU found a welcome mat in Kansas City, and it all started with Buchanan.

"That was the only trade I ever made for the franchise—Cotton Davidson to the Oakland Raiders for their No. 1 draft choice," Hunt said. "So I can retire with a 100 percent hit rate. I can say that every player I ever acquired made the Hall of Fame."

Bobby Bell

8

Bobby Bell grew up riding in the back of the bus.

That was a way of life for an African American child in North Carolina in the 1950s. A segregated South directed Bell to use restrooms and water fountains designated for "coloreds." He went to an all-Black school in Shelby, North Carolina, with only 170 students from first through twelfth grade. His high school was so small that Bell's team played six-man football. He was the quarterback—a state champion quarterback, an all-state quarterback.

But Blacks didn't play college football in the South back then. So the University of North Carolina or Duke University would not be on Bell's radar. The talented Black athlete had to go north to play, and the Big Ten was an inviting destination. The University of Minnesota got wind of Bell from his play in a high school All-Star Game and, sight unseen, offered him a scholarship.

When Bell left North Carolina to enroll at the University of Minnesota in 1959, it was the first time he had ever boarded an airplane. It was one of many firsts for Bell that year.

"The first time I ever played with white kids was when I went to Minnesota," Bell said. "Back then only 2 percent of the entire state was Black."

Bell dreamed of becoming the first African American quarterback to become an All-American. But one of his college teammates beat him there. Sandy Stephens led Minnesota to a national championship in 1960 to earn that acclaim in 1961. But the dream was still alive for Bell in 1959. Freshmen weren't eligible to play varsity, so Bell spent his first fall on campus as a quarterback of the scout team.

With Stephens entrenched as quarterback, though, the Minnesota Golden Gophers moved Bell from the backfield to the offensive line.

Entering his sophomore year, he was listed as a tackle. Bell moved there willingly.

"I told coach, 'I'm not going home. I can play any position. If you can coach me, I can play there,'" Bell recalled.

Bell was right—he could play there. Anywhere, in fact, the coaches wanted him to play. He spent his final three college seasons as a lineman, playing tackle both on offense and defense. He even doubled as the team's deep snapper on kicking downs his final two seasons.

There wasn't a better lineman in the country than Bell in his senior season in 1962. There were only a select few players better than him at any position in college football that year. Bell won the Outland Trophy as the nation's best lineman and finished third in the Heisman Trophy voting behind a quarterback (Terry Baker of Oregon State) and a running back (Jerry Stovall of LSU).

"I finished third, and Lee Roy Jordan was fourth or fifth," Bell said. "Years later a writer told me I got more votes for the Heisman than Baker . . . but Ernie Davis got it the year before. They weren't going to give another Black the Heisman Trophy. He was the first Black Heisman Trophy winner."

Bell had become a favorite son of the great state of Minnesota, and the NFL had every intention of keeping him there. Bell became a second-round draft choice of the Minnesota Vikings, the 16th overall selection of the 1963 draft. He was seemingly an afterthought in the AFL draft, going to the Dallas Texans in the seventh round.

"Everyone thought I would stay in Minnesota," Bell said. "My (college) coach Murray Warmath told me I needed to get a guaranteed contract from the Vikings. He said, 'They'll give you a three-year contract—but make sure they guarantee it.' So when I talked to (Vikings coach Norm) Van Brocklin, I asked for the guarantee. He said, 'We'll give you three years, but we don't guarantee contracts."

In the meantime, the Dallas Texans were becoming a looming presence. The club owner personally visited Bell in Minneapolis.

"Lamar Hunt came up to meet with me and asked me if I knew of a good ice cream place," Bel said. "Lamar loved ice cream. So I took him down on University Avenue, and we ate some ice cream. He said, 'I don't know what it's going to take, but I'd like you to be part of my family.'"

This was personal for Hunt. Four years earlier, as the founder of the American Football League, he granted Max Winter a franchise for Minneapolis. But before the AFL could even stage a training camp, Winter and the Minneapolis market were lured away by the NFL, leaving a sour taste in Hunt's mouth. Now Hunt wanted to take something away from the NFL and Max Winter that the Minneapolis market wanted: the Gophers' two-time All-American Bobby Bell.

Bell made one more pass at the Vikings. He showed up at a Wednesday practice in December hoping to talk with Van Brocklin. Bell's advisers told him he should sign a contract before December 31 for tax purposes—he needed to get that signing bonus in 1962 because if he signed to play in 1963 he would move into a different tax bracket. That day on the practice field, Bell was ready to sign.

But the Vikings weren't. Van Brocklin told him, "We won't be able to do this (right now) . . . but I got you covered."

Except that he didn't. Hunt returned to Minneapolis that week and sat down with Bell and his advisers.

"Lamar said, 'What's it going to take?'" Bell explained. "He gave me a longer-term contract and he personally guaranteed it. Then he asked me, 'Do we have a deal?' I said, 'Yes.' He didn't have a contract with him but said, 'Then we've got a deal.' He stood up and shook my hand and that of my two advisers. We said, 'What about the contract?' He said, 'Oh, I'll send you one and do whatever you have to do with it.' We basically wrote the contract, sent it back to him, and he signed it."

But unbeknownst to Hunt, he was signing a part-time player. And unbeknownst even to Bell, for that matter.

Bell would never play a down for the Dallas Texans. That's because after signing with the AFL the Texans would bolt Dallas for Kansas City to become the Chiefs.

As Bell was learning his way around his new town that spring, friends encouraged him to apply for an executive position at the General Motors Fairfax facility in Kansas City. As mentioned earlier, professional football players only worked six months out of the year. Most needed a supplemental income during the six-month offseason to help pay the bills. As a rookie, Bell qualified as among the needy. So he applied at GM—and was hired in the labor relations department.

"I worked full-time for GM," Bell said. "My second job was the Chiefs."

Bell spent six months out of the year with the Chiefs but twelve months with General Motors. He worked regular hours during the offseason, then took vacation during training camp. During the season, if the Chiefs practiced in the mornings, Bell would head off to General Motors in the afternoons to put in his hours. If the Chiefs practiced later in the day, Bell would show up at Fairfax at 5:00 a.m. to get his hours in. GM was flexible with Bell.

Bell was very good at what he did on the football field, finishing third in the AFL Rookie of the Year balloting in 1963. But he was also very good at what he did at his desk at General Motors. Twice he was offered promotions to the automaker's world headquarters in Detroit—and twice he turned GM down.

"They didn't know who I was," Bell said. "So finally the guy at GM said, 'Who is this Bell guy that keeps turning down promotions?' My guy down here said, 'You want to meet him?' So they came down, and when he saw me, the guy went, 'You're Bobby Bell . . . the football player? Oh, hell, they don't know that back there.'"

Bell would work twelve years for General Motors and was offered only one more promotion—to the Fremont facility in the Bay Area, just down the road from Oakland. Bell turned that offer down as well.

"I wasn't going to play for the Raiders," he said.

Bell certainly wasn't going to walk away from his football career. He was voted to the AFL All-Star Game in his second season in 1964—and each of the eight years thereafter. And he wasn't going to walk away from his other full-time gig either. Bell spent his entire twelve years at GM juggling football with cars.

Bell was no longer sitting in the back of the bus. He was now in the driver's seat of two careers.

9 The AFL West

The move to Kansas City was unsettling, to say the least, and the Chiefs never quite recovered from the relocation process.

The Chiefs added some cornerstone players in the 1963 draft in Buck Buchanan, guard Ed Budde, linebacker Bobby Bell, punter Jerrel Wilson, and tackle Dave Hill. But the effort to further upgrade the lines was dashed when Kansas City's second-, third-, and fourth-round draft picks—offensive tackle Walter Rock, defensive end Don Brumm, and guard Daryl Sanders—all signed with the NFL.

The crowds were bigger in Kansas City—the first five home crowds all topped twenty-five thousand—but the Chiefs were out of the divisional race before the first snowfall. Kansas City won only two of its first eleven games and watched both San Diego and Oakland zoom past the defending AFL champions in the West. San Diego finished 11–3, Oakland 10–4, with Kansas City a distant third at 5-7-2. The Chiefs went 0–4 against the Chargers and Raiders.

The Chargers lured quarterback Tobin Rote back from Canada that season. Rote had been a Pro Bowler for the Green Bay Packers in 1956 and then quarterbacked the Detroit Lions to an NFL championship in 1957. But he spent 1960–62 playing for the Toronto Argonauts of the Canadian Football League.

San Diego coach Sid Gillman convinced Rote to return south of the border where he would find a wide-open passing attack waiting for him with the Chargers. Gillman-Rote was as formidable a combination as Rote-Alworth. Rote and wide receiver Lance Alworth finished 1–2 in the AFL Player of the Year voting with Rote throwing for twenty touchdowns and winning the AFL passing crown. Alworth averaged 19.8 yards per his sixty-one receptions with eleven touchdowns.

Rote then threw a pair of touchdowns passes to power the Chargers to a 51–10 victory over the Boston Patriots in the AFL title game.

Al Davis arrived in Oakland in 1963 as head coach and general manager with his "commitment to excellence." Inside of one season, the Raiders charted a nine-game turnaround, improving from 1–13 in 1962 to that 10–4 mark in 1963, earning him AFL Coach of the Year honors. The Raiders defeated the Chiefs twice within a six-day span in November—and suddenly Kansas City had an archrival.

"When Al came in in 1963, we had just won the championship," Hank Stram said. "We were a big team, so Al drafted big people. He took Gene Upshaw so he could have someone to block Buck Buchanan. That was the way he built his team. He got Ray Guy because we had Jerrel Wilson. When Guy came out, I was toying with the idea of drafting him just so Al wouldn't get him. We would have kept Jerrel Wilson and traded Guy. That's how the competition was.

"You can't win big unless you can beat the competition in your own division. We both tried to get the same people. We tried to get Willie Brown from Denver, and the Raiders got him. Denver was reluctant to trade anyone to us because we always beat them. We played them thirty times in my fifteen years and we beat them twenty-six times. They were always reluctant to trade anyone to us. They felt the Raiders could help them knock us off. We tried to get Hewritt Dixon (from Denver) and he went to the Raiders too."

One of the biggest stars in the AFL galaxy was Buffalo running back Cookie Gilchrist, the AFL MVP in 1962 and league rushing champion in both 1962 and 1964. Stram wanted him to pair in the backfield with Dawson.

"So I called (Buffalo general manager) Dick Gallagher and told him I wanted Cookie," Stram said. "He said he couldn't trade him to us because, 'You beat us all the time, and I'd get run out of town if I traded him to you.' Furthermore, the Raiders were trying to get him too.

"We went back and forth, and finally I got a call from Scotty Sterling (of the Raiders). He said, 'Coach, Al Davis wants me to call to tell you if you lay off Gilchrist, we'll lay off Gilchrist. Would you be interested in that?' I thought about it, thinking that if we say yes they'd suck him right up. I figured this was one way to figure out what kind of guy Al really was, so I said, 'Okay fine.'

"The next day Dick Gallagher calls me and says, 'Coach, I've been thinking about this very seriously and the more I do, the more I'd like to see you have Cookie. I'm going to trade Cookie to you.' Well, what happened was that the Raiders called Dick and told him the Raiders no longer wanted him. So I told him, 'Dick, I appreciate it very much, but this has gone on long enough, and I've decided to go in a different direction. So we're no longer interested in Cookie.' He said, 'You've got to be interested in him. You'll like him. He'll be great for your team.'

"That cemented our relationship. Al honored his word, and I honored mine. If he tells you he's going to do something, he'll do it. If he likes you, there's nothing in the world he won't do for you."

The Bills eventually traded Gilchrist to Denver in 1965.

Landing Ed Budde was a huge coup for the Chiefs in 1963. The Philadelphia Eagles drafted the Michigan State guard with the fourth overall pick of the NFL draft. Dallas took Budde eighth overall pick in the AFL draft. Then he had a dilemma—the two contract offers were identical. So Budde called up a friend, fellow Michigan State Spartan and fellow Detroiter, Norm Masters, who was in his seventh season as an offensive lineman with the Green Bay Packers.

"I told Norm I needed to run something past him," Budde explained. "I said the Eagles and Chiefs offered me the same thing—$8,000 (signing bonus) and $15,000 a year. There was about a five-second hesitation, and I said, 'Norm, are you still there?' He said, 'Yes. Hey, I'm only making $14,000, and I've been in the league for seven years. Sign a contract now before anyone changes their mind.'"

Then Budde made a second call to another friend, fellow Spartan and fellow Detroiter—Fred Arbanas, a tight end with the Texans.

"He said it was a new league, a more exciting league, more wide-open league with more passing," Budde said. "He talked about 'Bambi' (Lance Alworth) and all these great receivers. Then I was impressed with what I saw when I went down there."

Robinson, Spikes, Holub, Tyrer, Buchanan, Budde—the Chiefs were administering some major licks on the NFL in the signing wars. Kansas

City continued to set its sights high, showing a willingness to compete financially for the best college players in the land. The Chiefs drafted Heisman Trophy winner Roger Staubach in 1964 and running back Gale Sayers and linebacker Mike Curtis in 1965. But the Chiefs lost Staubach to the Cowboys, Sayers to the Bears, and Curtis to the Colts. Staubach and Sayers became Hall of Famers and Curtis a Pro Bowler.

Not only were the Chiefs falling short of adding quality players in 1964 and 1965 but they were also losing star players of their own.

Arbanas was the top tight end in the AFL, having been voted to the league All-Star Game three consecutive seasons from 1962–64. But in December 1964, Arbanas was mugged on a Kansas City street and lost the sight of his left eye.

"I figured my career as a football player was all over at that point in time," Arbanas said, "and that I'd probably have to go back home to Detroit and work in a factory or teach school."

But before Arbanas could hire a moving van, he received a call from Stram in February.

"I can remember like it was yesterday," Arbanas said. "It was cold, and there was snow on the ground. Hank was all excited, and he says to me, 'Don't worry about it. You can still play football. I just had Stu and Dale (his sons) and the rest of the kids out in the front yard, and we all had patches over one eye. We were throwing the ball around, and we would catch it. I know darn well if we can catch it, you can catch it.' I knew right then and there Hank was going to give me a good shot at coming back."

Arbanas may have been on the verge of walking away from football but Stram had no intention of walking away from Arbanas.

"It would have been easy to say, 'No, you can't play anymore,'" Stram said. "Anybody could have done that. The real challenge was to somehow find a way for him to play. You've got to find a way to keep those great players playing."

Fullback Mack Lee Hill was one of the best success stories in the early days of the Chiefs. He signed as an undrafted college free agent from Southern in 1964 and won a starting position that season. He rushed for 567 yards, averaging 5.4 yards per carry, and was voted to the AFL All-Star Game.

Hill was even better in 1965 with 627 rushing yards before suffering a knee injury in the thirteenth game of the season at Buffalo.

"Mack was sitting next to me on the flight back home and said, 'Jerry, I know they are going to do surgery on this knee,'" tackle Jerry Cornelison explained. "I said, 'Mack, you don't know that yet. This just happened a few hours ago.' He said, 'Yeah, but it hurts, and it's all swollen up. I just know they are going to do surgery—and I'm scared to death of surgeries.' I said, 'Oh, Mack, don't worry about it. You'll be okay."

Hill died on the operating table two days later from complications during the surgery. Despite having played for Kansas City less than two seasons, the Chiefs retired his No. 36 jersey and to this day present their top rookie each season with the Mack Lee Hill Award.

"Mack was one of the truly exciting players we've ever had in a Chiefs' uniform," Hunt said. "He played with incredible spirit and was the first great star developed in Kansas City. We brought some stars here, people who won a championship in Dallas, but they sort of fell flat on their faces in 1963. Then Mack Lee Hill arrived in 1964. He was the beginning of the Kansas City player. He's still the greatest short-yardage player I ever saw. He could explode into the line and move a stack of players."

On the field, the Chiefs were the personification of AFL mediocrity, posting a 19-19-4 record those first three years in Kansas City. Not only had the Texans lost their identity when they left Texas, they lost their swagger.

The Merger 10

There may not have been a more competitive person in the AFL than Al Davis. So his disdain for the Kansas City Chiefs was understandable.

In 1963, when he was thirty-four, Davis was named head coach of the Oakland Raiders. The previous season, the Raiders finished at the bottom of the league with a 1–13 record. The Dallas Texans—soon to be the Chiefs—were atop the AFL with an 11–3 record and the championship trophy. The Chiefs were big, strong, fast, and had the league's best quarterback: Len Dawson. The Chiefs were all that Davis wanted his Raiders to be—and Kansas City was now standing in his way in the Western Division.

In the short term, Davis wanted to take the Chiefs down. But he also had a long-term goal—take the entire NFL down.

"I loved the AFL," Davis said. "It was a young league. It was meaningful to me. Even when I was in the American Football League, I had opportunities to go to the National Football League. But I wouldn't take them. With no disrespect, I'll say it—I thought they were arrogant. I wasn't afraid of them. We thought we could beat them without any trouble."

The AFL was cherry-picking some NFL draft picks—but the majority of the top college players was still signing with the older league. However, the perception of the AFL started to change in 1964 when the league signed a five-year, $36 million deal with NBC for broadcast rights. That gave the AFL a blank check to aggressively hunt down players.

The New York Jets then rocked the NFL by signing Alabama quarterback Joe Namath a day after his final college appearance in the Orange Bowl to the richest contract ever for a rookie in any sport—$427,000 over three years. Davis himself signed Florida State All-American wide receiver Fred Biletnikoff under the goalposts after he caught four touchdowns against Oklahoma in the Gator Bowl.

That spending certainly got the attention of NFL players.

"It was exciting from the potential of salary standpoint," Green Bay's Pro Bowl guard Jerry Kramer said. "It was going to have an impact on salaries almost immediately with certain players. Eventually you had some hopes that it would impact your salary. We had our Gold Dust twins in (Jim) Grabowski and (Donny) Anderson. They were making in the $300,000–$500,000 range, whereas Bart (Starr) was making in the $35,000 range, Paul probably $35,000, and Jimmy $30,000. The huge salaries were an immediate topic of conversation."

The AFL's focus shifted from survival to becoming an actual rival of the NFL. And who better to lead the charge against the NFL than Davis, who was named the commissioner of the AFL in April 1966. Some of the AFL owners were hoping Davis could force a merger with the NFL. But not Al—he wanted to bring the NFL to its knees.

And there was a faction of AFLers who believed he could do it.

"I don't know that there's a greater competitor in the world than Al Davis," Hank Stram said. "Nobody in the world wants to win more than he does. Nobody will pay more of a price than he does. His whole life is football."

Davis grew up in Brooklyn and set up his AFL office in New York.

"[NFL commissioner Pete] Rozelle was in fear of me," Davis said. "There was pandemonium. We had taken over New York. We had a press conference, and everyone was excited. I had made the statement I didn't give a care about the other league. We can beat them head-to-head. We can out-recruit them. We've out-signed them already.

"Howard Cosell, sitting right up front, asked about the disaster in Denver and another city. I said I'm going to name eight of those cities in the other league, and you're going to have to agree that they're a bigger disaster than those two."

A month after setting up shop, Davis flew to Detroit to confer with Ralph Wilson, the owner of the Buffalo Bills and the president of the American Football League. While Davis was in Detroit, Wilson received a shocking phone call—the New York Giants had signed away his place-kicker Pete Gogolak. He became the first star AFL player to defect to the NFL.

"I told Ralph, 'You just got a merger,'" Davis said. "He said, 'What do you mean? Gogolak just signed.' He was incensed. I said, 'You've got a merger, don't worry about it.'"

Davis returned to New York with a plan—if you're going to take our players, we're going to take yours.

"It was pretty obvious they (the NFL) had a lot of players that wanted to leave," Davis said. "They wanted to come over to the new league. One of them I knew very well from the Green Bay Packers—Willie Wood, who played for me at Southern Cal. He was with Herb Adderley, who was from Philadelphia. I knew him when he was in high school. The plan was pretty simple. It was brinkmanship, putting the fear of God in them."

The AFL plotted to sign NFL players to future contracts. The NFLers could play out the final year of their existing NFL contracts in 1966 and then change leagues in 1967. Davis established some targets—quarterbacks Roman Gabriel, John Brodie, and Jim Ninowski, tight end Mike Ditka . . .

"There were about eight of them," Davis said. "I didn't need to draw up a list. Everyone was vulnerable."

Davis did indeed put the fear of God in the NFL. Within a month of the Gogolak signing, the two leagues had announced a merger. The AFL agreed to pay $18 million to the NFL as indemnification because two AFL teams would be sharing markets with NFL teams: New York and San Francisco.

"I thought the merger was excellent," Davis said. "But I didn't like the terms of it, giving all that money to them. For what? They pulled a fast one. They wanted to go sixteen (NFL teams) and ten (AFL teams)—keep our league separate. I said, 'No, we're going thirteen and thirteen.' I forced that. So Art Modell, the Rooneys, and Carroll Rosenbloom saw an easy way to pick up $3 million, and they came over to our league."

Modell was the owner of the Cleveland Browns, Art Rooney was the owner of the Pittsburgh Steelers, and Rosenbloom owned the Baltimore Colts. They agreed to change affiliation to the AFL to facilitate the merger and balance out the two conferences. As Davis noted, they were paid handsomely for their transfer in allegiance.

But the merger also cost Davis his job. Pete Rozelle would become the commissioner of the combined leagues when the merger officially took place in 1970. So Davis returned to the Raiders in the summer of 1966 as a part owner and the head of football operations.

Under terms of the merger, the NFL would become the National Football Conference (NFC) and the AFL the American Football Conference (AFC) in 1970. But the two leagues would begin playing a "world championship game" at the end of the 1966 season and then they would move to a series of exhibition games in 1967.

The NFL always downplayed the impact of Davis on the merger, maintaining that the wheels were already in motion with clandestine talks in Dallas between AFL founder Lamar Hunt and Cowboys president Tex Schramm.

"Thirty years from now they'll probably say (Norman) Schwarzkopf had nothing to do with the Persian Gulf." Davis smirked.

And suddenly, teams in non-NFL markets—Boston, Buffalo, Denver, Houston, Kansas City, and San Diego—had the chance to play for a world championship.

11 Mike Garrett

Mike Garrett was as Los Angeles as the Sunset Strip.

Garrett was born in the City of Angels, grew up there, played high school and college football there, and fully expected to play professional football there.

The University of Southern California (USC) has a well-earned reputation as Tailback U. The Trojans have produced ten All-American tailbacks, including five Heisman Trophy winners. But before there was a Reggie Bush, a Marcus Allen, a Charles White, or an O.J. Simpson, there was Mike Garrett. He's the godfather of the Tailback U tradition, winning the Heisman in 1965 after rushing for 1,440 yards and scoring thirteen touchdowns.

The Downtown Athletic Club informed Garrett that he had won the Heisman on November 23, 1965—and four days later the AFL and NFL both conducted their 1966 college drafts. Garrett gave both leagues something to think about that same day by rushing for 112 yards and three touchdowns in his final college game, a 56–6 trouncing of the University of Wyoming.

The Los Angeles Rams coveted Garrett for two obvious reasons: first, to plug college football's best running back into their own backfield, and second, to keep him away from the AFL. The two leagues agreed to a merger seven months later, so the 1966 draft would be the last time the AFL and NFL would compete financially for players.

But there was one hitch.

"The draft was chaotic back then," Garrett said. "Nobody was following any rules. The Rams told me (beforehand) they would draft me No. 1 but only if I agreed to sign with them. So I told them, 'That would take all my negotiating power away.' So they drafted me No. 2."

That didn't figure to be an obstacle for the Rams—not after watching Garrett tumble to the 20th round of the AFL draft to the Kansas City Chiefs on their final pick. His slide was logical—no one expected the hometown hero to leave his hometown in pursuit of a professional football career. And that included Garrett himself.

Until Garrett bumped into Southern Cal coach John McKay the following week, that is. McKay played college football at Purdue where he had been a teammate of Hank Stram. The Chiefs needed to find someone to replace their Pro Bowl running back, the late Mack Lee Hill, and Stram talked to McKay about Garrett. The Chiefs missed out on Gale Sayers in 1965 and had no intention of missing out on Garrett in 1966.

"My lawyer said the Chiefs told him they would treat me as a No. 1 if I was willing to negotiate with them," Garrett said. "I said, sure. The Rams offered me No. 2 money. The Chiefs offered me substantially more. I never knew why the Rams took the position they took. My agent told me, 'I think you're going to be a Chief.'"

And for the third time in seven drafts, the AFL signed the Heisman Trophy winner away from the NFL—Billy Cannon in 1959, Notre Dame's John Huarte in 1964, and Garrett in 1965. Garrett was leaving the most famous football building in the nation—the Los Angeles Coliseum—to play his professional football in a forty-thousand-seat baseball stadium in the middle of nowhere.

"I didn't know a damn thing about Kansas City," Garrett said. "I remember going to William Jewell College for training camp and just trying to figure out, 'Where am I? This is the Midwest . . . What's this all about?'

"But I remember looking at all the players we had from all over the country—most of them seemed to be from the HBCU—and just trying to figure out how good they were. We had guys from Michigan State, Ohio State . . . plus guys from Bethune Cookman, Grambling. I thought this is amazing that the AFL made it possible for such a mixture of talent. Black, white . . . we had more Blacks on our team than anybody in either league. It was remarkable. And the town was electric."

The town wasn't generating the only electricity in Kansas City. So were the Chiefs.

"I followed some of the AFL teams, but I wasn't familiar with Kansas City," Garrett said. "When I got here I thought, 'Oh my God—these guys are good. I didn't know about Otis Taylor before I got here. I didn't know about Buck Buchanan. We had good players. We felt we could play with anybody."

But the Chiefs still had to prove it to their fans. Since moving from Dallas to Kansas City in 1963, the Chiefs had become an AFL also-ran, watching the San Diego Chargers win three consecutive Western Division titles. The Chiefs were coming off a 7-5-2 season and a third-place finish in the West in 1965. The starting lineup was returning intact except for three players.

The Chiefs lost wide receiver Frank Jackson and defensive end Mel Branch to the Miami Dolphins in the AFL expansion, so Otis Taylor replaced Jackson, and Chuck Hurston stepped in for Branch. Garrett moved into the offensive backfield in place of Mack Lee Hill.

How much of a difference could three players make?

"I remember when I went to USC as a freshman and people wondered, 'Can USC come back?'" Garrett said. "And we did. I felt the same way going to Kansas City. After being around the guys in camp and seeing the talent we had, I thought, 'Oh my God, we could hurt somebody.'"

Just twelve months earlier, Garrett wasn't even sure his future would be in football. He also played college baseball and was drafted three times—twice by his hometown Los Angeles Dodgers, once as high as the fourth round.

"Football was easier for me but at my size (five-nine, 190 lbs) I probably could get away with it better in baseball," Garrett said. "So I wasn't sure how it was going to play out. But after my senior year, I was interested to see how I could do in the NFL. People had been talking trash about my size. But after that first scrimmage at William Jewell, I thought to myself, 'I can play here.'"

And Garrett would go on to prove it.

Fig. 1. Wide receiver Chris Burford (88) is upended after a catch against the Packers in the first Super Bowl

Fig. 2. Defensive end Chuck Hurston

Fig. 3. Defensive tackle Curley Culp

Fig. 4. Fullback Jack Spikes

Fig. 5. Wide receiver Otis Taylor

Fig. 6. Linebacker E. J. Holub in pregame introductions at Kansas City's Municipal Stadium

Fig. 7. Middle linebacker Willie Lanier

Fig. 8. Receivers Chris Burford (88), Otis Taylor (89), and Fred Arbanas (84)

Fig. 9. Kansas City safeties Johnny Robinson (42) and Bobby Hunt (20)

Fig. 10. Guard Ed Budde (71)

Fig. 11. Otis Taylor draws up a play in the dirt for quarterback Len Dawson at the Kansas City bench

Fig. 12. Offensive tackle Dave Hill

Fig. 13. Offensive tackle Dave Hill (73) and safety Bobby Hunt (20)

Fig. 14. Defensive end Jerry Mays

Fig. 15. Linebacker Sherrill Headrick (69) tackles San Diego halfback Paul Lowe (23) in an AFL game

Fig. 16. Linebacker Bobby Bell (78)

Fig. 17. Halfback Mike Garrett (21) eludes a tackle against the Oakland Raiders

Fig. 18. Receivers Otis Taylor (89) and Fred Arbanas (84) on the Kansas City sideline

Fig. 19. Coach Hank Stram (L) and scout Lloyd Wells

Fig. 20. Owner Lamar Hunt at a preseason banquet in Kansas City

Fig. 21. Quarterback Cotton Davidson (19) throws a pass to Johnny Robinson (42) in the Dallas Texans/empty seat days

Fig. 22. Owner Lamar Hunt speaking at a press conference in Kansas City

The Buffalo Bills 12

A golden opportunity awaited the Buffalo Bills in 1966.

In 1959 the city of Buffalo was the twentieth largest in the United States. There were sixteen Major League Baseball teams then, and all had been around for decades. There were twelve National Football League teams, and most of them had been around for decades. A small-market town like Buffalo had no hope of ever cracking either fraternity.

Then the AFL came along in 1960—but Buffalo remained an afterthought even for that league. Ralph Wilson was granted one of the eight franchises and hoped to place his team in Miami. But he couldn't come to terms on a lease with the Orange Bowl, so Wilson decided his team would play just a short hop from his home office in Detroit—Buffalo.

The Bills would scuffle along in their first three seasons competing in the four-team Eastern Division, losing more games (twenty-two) than they won (eighteen) and never finishing higher than third place with a different quarterback each season—Johnny Green in 1960, M. C. Reynolds in 1961, and Warren Rabb in 1962.

Then the San Diego Chargers made a critical mistake by trying to slide injured quarterback Jack Kemp through waivers early in the 1962 season with the purpose of stashing him until a broken finger could heal. But the quarterback-needy Bills upset that strategy by claiming Kemp for a mere one-hundred-dollar waiver fee. Buffalo would patiently wait for his finger to mend to add the two-time AFL All-Star quarterback to its huddle.

Kemp promptly delivered the Bills their first playoff berth in 1963, passing for 2,910 yards and thirteen touchdowns. Buffalo tied the Boston Patriots for first place in the East with 7-6-1 records, and the two met in an elimination game for the right to play San Diego for the AFL championship. The Patriots prevailed, 26–8, but were trampled by the Chargers, 51–10.

But no one could deny the Bills in 1964—or 1965, for that matter. The Bills posted a 12–2 record in 1964, then crushed the Chargers 20–7 in the AFL title game. Buffalo finished 10-3-1 in 1965 and again pummeled the Chargers, 23–0, for back-to-back championships.

The Bills were stacked in 1964, stacked in 1965, and would be stacked again in 1966. Buffalo had the league's best player and best defense. Stay on top one more season and the Bills would be playing in the inaugural AFL-NFL championship game.

The AFL owners may have wanted the merger and the championship game between the two leagues. But not all the players were on board. Al Davis wasn't the only AFL mind that thought his league had the NFL on the run.

"I thought the AFL was pretty much on par with the NFL," Buffalo cornerback Booker Edgerson said. "In fact, I thought the AFL was more in the spotlight because of the way we played the game. It was fast, exciting—it was like MTV football. People really enjoyed watching the high-caliber of players we had, most of whom could have played in the NFL.

"The NFL was a slow, boring league. I wish they had not merged at that particular time. I was hoping it wouldn't happen. I understand it was all about the money and the prestige. But I felt we had already established ourselves. We weren't going to go away. I think we would have been a greater force in the eyes of the fans had we not merged."

Pete Gogolak was just one of the many AFL's innovations that would forever change the game. He was the first soccer-style kicker to play professional football—and he was playing for the Bills. Buffalo made him a 12th-round pick in 1964, and Gogolak rewarded the team's faith in him with consecutive 100-point seasons. His 102 points in 1964 helped the Bills win their first AFL title, and his 115 points in 1965 helped them go back-to-back. Gogolak was voted to his first—and as it turns out, only—AFL All-Star Game that season.

That's because the New York Giants signed Gogolak that offseason. He became the AFL's first homegrown star to jump to the NFL. And that made the Bills the tip of the spear for the merger. But even without Gogolak, the Bills remained the team to beat in the AFL in 1966.

Kemp was the reigning AFL MVP, and one of eight Bills named first-team All-AFL along with guard Billy Shaw, defensive end Ron McDole, defensive tackle Tom Sestak, outside linebacker Mike Stratton, cornerback Butch Byrd, safety George Saimes, and Gogolak. In addition, offensive tackle Stew Barber, defensive end Tom Day, defensive tackle Jim Dunaway, middle linebacker Harry Jacobs, and outside backer John Tracey were all voted to the second team.

The Buffalo roster would be fortified in 1966 with the return of star receiver Elbert "Golden Wheels" Dubenion. He caught forty-two passes for 1,139 yards—a staggering 27.1-yard average—with ten touchdowns in 1964 but suffered a season-ending knee injury in the third game of the 1965 season.

Another touchdown maker was added to the mix in running back Bobby Burnett, who scored sixteen of them as a senior at the University of Arkansas in 1965. He was a fourth-round draft selection, the highest choice signed by the Bills that offseason.

But the three-peat train ran off the tracks in the 1966 season opener when the AFL scheduled a rematch of the 1965 championship game in San Diego. This time the Chargers did the spanking, steamrolling the Bills, 27–7. This was against a defense that allowed the fewest points in the AFL the previous season, an average of only 16.1 per game.

But it was even worse the next week—at home, yet—when the Chiefs trounced the Bills, 42–20. Those were the most points allowed by Buffalo in a game since 1961 when Boston put 52 on the scoreboard. Those were the most points the Bills allowed at home since 1960 when the same Kansas City franchise, this time dressed as the Dallas Texans, smacked them around for 45. It also marked the first time the Bills had lost back-to-back games since 1963.

Then the football gods intervened.

The AFL expanded to nine teams in 1966, adding the Miami Dolphins and placing them in the Eastern Division. The Dolphins stocked their roster in the expansion draft with older players left unprotected by their AFL teams, including wide receiver Frank Jackson of the Chiefs, tight end Dave Kocourek of the Chargers, and linebacker Wahoo McDaniel from the Jets. The Dolphins used their first-round draft pick on All-American fullback Jim Grabowski of Illinois but failed to sign him. He opted for the defending NFL champion Green Bay Packers. Miami's primary quarterback that season was the son of the head coach, George Wilson.

Joe Auer returned the opening kickoff of the season 95 yards for a Miami touchdown, but it was all downhill from there. The Dolphins won only three games that season and would be no match for the elite teams of the AFL.

Starting in week three at Buffalo, the Bills ended their losing ways with a 58–24 dismantling of the Dolphins. The Bills never scored more points in a game before or since. Golden Wheels made his presence felt with five catches for 101 yards, but it was cornerback Butch Byrd who would carry Buffalo that day. He returned an interception 60 yards for one touchdown and carried a punt back 72 yards for another, both in the first quarter.

The Bills were competitive on offense that season with Kemp throwing the ball to Dubenion and handing it to Burnett and fullback Wray Carlton. But it was the defense and kicking game that made Buffalo special. The Bills finished second in scoring that season in the AFL with 358 points—but 54 of them came when the offense was off the field. Buffalo returned four interceptions, two punts, a kickoff, a fumble, and a blocked field goal for touchdowns as the Bills won nine of their last twelve games to capture a third consecutive Eastern Division crown.

Offensively, the Bills did not register a single 300-yard passing day all season from Kemp. Buffalo managed only two 100-yard receiving days (both by Dubenion) and one 100-yard rusher (Burnett). But when your defense is allowing a league-low of 255 points, your offense doesn't need to be superhuman.

The Bills held five of their opponents to 14 points or less. That included a shutout of the Dolphins in November and keeping Joe Namath and the Jets out of the end zone a week later. That Buffalo defense intercepted twenty-nine passes, recovered ten fumbles, and allowed an average of only 75 yards per game on the ground, easily the best in the AFL.

Because the AFL alternated the site of its championship game each year, it was the East's turn to host the title game in 1966—and the right to represent the AFL in what would become the first "Super Bowl."

The Bills had a Rockpile awaiting their Western Division challenger.

Hank Stram 13

The AFL gave George Blanda, Jack Kemp, Babe Parilli, Frank Tripucka, and Al Dorow the chance to do something that they never got the chance to do in the NFL.

Air it out.

All were NFL castoffs who became starting quarterbacks in the AFL's inaugural season in 1960. All embraced the fledgling league's aerial philosophy.

The NFL had one 3,000-yard passer in 1960 and only two others in its thirteen-team league who threw for as many as 2,000 yards. The AFL had two 3,000-yard passers that season and four other quarterbacks in its eight-team league that threw for at least 2,000 yards. The following season Blanda set an American pro football record with thirty-six touchdown passes.

The NFL remained a league powered by legs at the turn of the 1960 decade. Jim Brown, John David Crow, Paul Hornung, J.D. Smith, Jim Taylor, and Nick Pietrosante remained the feature attractions on the NFL's marquee. The NFL loved to run the football. Everyone in the AFL loved to throw it.

Well, almost everyone.

Then there was Hank Stram. A Big Tenner at heart with his Purdue diploma, Stram believed success on the football field started on the ground.

Which is why Stram stocked his shelves in 1960 with three backs each capable of 100 rushing yards on any given Sunday for the Texans—halfbacks Abner Haynes and Johnny Robinson and fullback Jack Spikes.

The fullback position was not the afterthought then as it has become in today's NFL, filled with lead blockers and pass catchers. Fullbacks in the 1950s and 1960s were expected to carry both their weight on offense and the football. NFL fullbacks won thirteen consecutive rushing titles from 1953 through 1965.

If "Ground Hank" hoped to succeed in the AFL, Stram knew he needed a pounder to complement his two gliders at halfback. Which is why he traded a projected starting safety (Austin Gonsoulin) to Denver for Spikes following the first AFL draft.

"I don't think there's any question that you have to have a big, strong fullback—a durable guy who can dance every dance, who can play all sixteen games," Stram said. "I always felt you need thunder and lightning—that big fullback who can get the tough yardage inside and also the halfback who could get to the outside."

The Texans were one of two teams to rush for 2,000 yards in 1960, finishing second to the Oakland Raiders. But Dallas did rush for a league-best twenty-four touchdowns. The Texans were the only team to rush for 2,000 yards in 1961 and one of only two teams to get there again in 1962. Haynes finished first in the AFL in rushing in 1960, third in 1961, and second in 1962 with the first 1,000-yard season in franchise history.

All the while, Stram continued to eye his shelves. He drafted fullback Curtis McClinton in 1961 and another fullback—Baylor All-American Ronnie Bull—with a first-round draft choice in 1962. But Bull elected to sign with the NFL. Stram drafted bruising halfback Joe Don Looney in 1964 but lost him to the NFL as well. He drafted halfback Gale Sayers and fullback Mike Curtis in 1965 but again lost out on both to the NFL. He drafted three more fullbacks in 1966, including Walt Garrison of Oklahoma State, as well as halfback Mike Garrett. He lost all three of his fullbacks but landed Garrett.

Even if you couldn't run the ball, the threat of the run always had to be there. And you needed backs to pose that threat, so Stram kept drafting them.

"The farther you go, the more balance you need to have," Stram said. "You can't win without good balance. You have to have a good running game, and it will open things up for your passing game. You have a good passing game, and it'll open things up for the running game. You don't win the Super Bowl with a one-dimensional attack or a one-phase personality."

Stram was called "Dapper" by his friends for his natty sideline attire. But he was dubbed "The Mentor" by his players because of his offensive creativity. Stram was always willing to stroll outside of the box.

His first major wrinkle was a formation from his college coaching days.

"We started using the I-formation in 1962 with Abner Haynes," Stram said. "We used it against Denver and beat them overwhelmingly (24–3). It was the first time the I-formation had ever been used in pro football. One of the most prominent coaches in the game—and I won't give you his name because he's a friend of mine—once told me, 'Dapper, that I-formation will never work in professional football. It's a college formation.'"

But Stram continued to use the I, and it continued to work for him. The arrival of quarterback Len Dawson in 1962 allowed Stram to hone his offensive philosophy even further. He remembered recruiting Dawson to Purdue and one of the major features in his game.

"Lenny was a magician," said Mel Knowlton, Dawson's high school coach. "He was cool and calm and worked on trying to fool people. The play-action pass was made for him."

With Dawson now in Stram's huddle, the play-action would become a staple of the Texans that fed off an already stout Dallas running game.

"We ran the ball so well that we felt play-action passes would give us extra time," Stram explained. "We had such big, strong offensive linemen like Ed Budde, David Hill, and Jim Tyrer. Lenny was an excellent faker, and we had small backs who were hidden by the fake in the backfield."

Dawson was all in on the philosophy. He understood he didn't need to throw the ball thirty times per game for the Texans to win. The Texans averaged twenty-three passes per game in 1962 on the way to their first AFL title. Dawson was willing to play to the strength of his offense.

"We had such a huge offensive line," Dawson said. "The worst thing they did was pass block. I had a lot of time because of the play-action pass. We had a running team. We could move the ball on the ground with those big old guys straight ahead."

Stram's next wrinkle was born out of necessity—the moving pocket.

"Our chief competition at the time was the San Diego Chargers," Stram said. "They had a tremendous defensive line with Earl Faison and Ernie Ladd. Those guys were huge and knocked down six to seven balls a game when you tried to throw from the pocket. The first time we used the moving pocket against San Diego, we beat them in the last game of the (1962) season. We used a lot of rollouts with the tight end blocking down on the defensive end. Lenny completed his first eleven passes of the game, and we won, 26–17. We did that out of necessity."

Like the play-action, the moving pocket was a perfect fit for the talents of Dawson, who was a tad shorter than the prototype for the quarterback position at 6-foot.

"We felt offenses should be like a pitcher's repertoire," Stram said. "You can't stay in the big leagues if you throw the fastball all the time. You need a curveball, a change of pace, a slider, a knuckler, whatever . . . You have to have a variety of pitches to keep the other guy off balance.

"From a passing standpoint we had quick passes with a three-step drop, pocket passes, play-action passes, and rollouts. We didn't want the defense to feel they knew where our quarterback would be every time he went back to pass. When he rolled right or left, he had all the time in the world, and he had much better vision. He didn't have to throw over all those giants. The days of the quarterback being a statue were over."

The Texans rushed for a franchise record with 2,407 yards in 1962. But Dawson also won his first AFL passing title that season with an efficiency rating of 98.3, leading the league with twenty-nine touchdown passes. He would win five more AFL passing titles in succession from 1964–68, which remains a pro football record fifty-six years later.

Stram had devised the perfect offense for the talent on his roster. He could run or pass by choice. He could toy with formations, lining up tight ends and wide receivers in the backfield. Stram would motion players and also run reverses and option passes with halfbacks, fullbacks, and even wide receivers throwing the ball.

"Everything we did was based on how we were going to best use our personnel," Stram said. "How are we going to do it better than everybody else? How are we going to get a little jump? How are we going to get a winning edge? The bottom line was this: How will this help us win? That's all, nothing else. If it will help us, let's do it and not worry about what anybody says or does."

There was one other factor in Stram's construction of a game plan each week: the opponent.

"One year the Raiders were playing the bump-and-run so great," Stram said. "They had David Grayson and George Atkinson, who were both fantastic cover guys but not real good tacklers. So we lined up in a full house—two tight ends and three backs—and only threw three passes in the game. We beat them badly in Kansas City. Al (Davis) was furious."

That was one of only two games the Raiders lost in that 1968 season. Dawson completed 2-of-3 passes for 16 yards but the Chiefs ran the ball sixty times for 294 yards and three touchdowns in a 24–10 triumph.

The NFL was still running the ball in 1966, and the AFL was still passing it. The Chiefs had the most diverse offense in football with the ability to dominate either on the ground or through the air. With all the motion and trickery at his disposal, Stram was giving fans a peek at what was to come in the game of football in the 1970s and 1980s.

"There are a lot of ways to get from here to Los Angeles," Stram said. "You can take an airplane, a train, a bus, a car, a motorcycle, a bicycle, a skateboard . . . Our offense was such that we wanted to take a jet. Some people at the time were taking the bus. But we felt it was a jet age, and we wanted to perform that way."

Stram wanted to get to Los Angeles by the end of the 1966 season. The Los Angeles Coliseum would be the site of the first AFL-NFL championship game. Stram would have two new toys to play with offensively in 1966: a new running back and an emerging wide receiver. Mike Garrett and Otis Taylor would provide Stram his boarding pass to the jet age.

14 Western Dominance

Everyone was tiring of the mediocrity on the football field in Kansas City by 1966—Lamar Hunt, Hank Stram, the players, and their fans.

The crowds of thirty thousand that welcomed the Chiefs in their first season in Kansas City in 1962 were long gone. Three consecutive seasons as an AFL also-ran would test the patience of even the most rabid fan base. And Kansas City was already a town beaten down by a decade of sporting mediocrity by the baseball A's. Only 14,421 bothered to show up for the 1965 finale when the Chiefs were closing out a 7-5-2 season with another third-place finish in the Western Division.

Then Kansas City absorbed some major roster hits in the offseason. The passing of Mack Lee Hill left a cavernous void in the offensive backfield, and Kansas City lost two more starters to the Miami Dolphins in the expansion draft: wide receiver Frank Jackson and defensive end Mel Branch.

Those three players went to a combined five AFL All-Star Games—Branch in 1961–63, Hill in 1964, and Jackson in 1965. Branch led the AFL with ten sacks in 1960 and gave the Chiefs eight more as his parting gift in 1965. Jackson led the Chiefs in receiving in 1964 and was among the AFL leaders with his nine touchdowns.

So Stram prepared to wander into the unknown, elevating three players with a combined four AFL career starts into the starting lineup of the 1966 Chiefs. The rookie Garrett would replace Hill, Taylor would step in for Jackson, and Chuck Hurston would take over for Branch. Taylor and Hurston were both rookies in 1965, with Taylor starting those four games, including three to close the season because of an injury to Chris Burford.

But that relative inexperience didn't show up at William Jewell College that summer. First the Texans and then the Chiefs had quality backs throughout their history. Abner Haynes, Hill, Jack Spikes, and Curtis McClinton all had 100-yard rushing games, and all but Spikes had been invited to the AFL All-Star Game. But the franchise had never seen the speed and quickness that the newcomer Garrett brought to the field. He was electric.

And Taylor . . . he was a revelation. The Chiefs couldn't cover him in training camp. He caught only twenty-six passes as a rookie but averaged 17.2 yards per reception with five touchdowns. There were flashes in 1965—but those flashes were now occurring daily in training camp. He would be among the toughest receivers Kansas City cornerbacks Willie Mitchell and Fred Williamson would face that season.

This had the potential to become the best offense Stram would field in franchise history. The Chiefs had eight starters who had already appeared in AFL All-Star Games: Len Dawson, Fred Arbanas, Ed Budde, Chris Burford, Jon Gilliam, Abner Haynes, Curtis McClinton, and Jim Tyrer. Garrett and Taylor showed the potential in August to one day join them. One day very soon.

For the first time since 1960, the Chiefs breezed through the exhibition season undefeated, bludgeoning Denver, Miami, San Diego, and Houston on consecutive weekends in August. Kansas City scored at least 31 points in all four of the victories. It was clear to Stram that the Chiefs would go as far as their offense could carry them. It was clear to everyone, in fact.

"If we lacked anything it was probably on defense," Garrett said. "Offensively we had Otis Taylor, myself, Chris Burford, Fred Arbanas . . . We could move the ball, and we could compete. The question was could we defense you."

The baseball A's had seniority on the Chiefs at Municipal Stadium, so they had first call on dates—and the A's held on to those weekend dates in September. So, for the second consecutive season and third time in four years, Kansas City opened with its first three games on the road. And the opener was in Buffalo against the two-time defending AFL champion, the Bills. The Chiefs had lost five consecutive games to the Bills and had not beaten them since 1962. The Chiefs also hadn't won a game in Buffalo since 1960.

In addition, Stram's explosive offense would face the AFL's most formidable defense in the opener: the Bills. Not only that but the Chiefs were off the first weekend of the AFL season, and this would be Buffalo's second game. The Bills had the benefit of having to review and clean up the issues from their own season opener: that 27–7 loss to the San Diego Chargers.

But Buffalo's defense got steamrolled. The Chiefs blasted the Bills, 42–20. Halfback Bert Coan rushed for 101 yards and a touchdown and also caught a 12-yard touchdown pass from Dawson. It was the first 100-yard rushing day against the Bills in thirty-five games dating to the 1963 season. McClinton also scored on both a run and a pass, Taylor caught a touchdown pass, and Garrett returned a punt 79 yards for another score.

The winning continued and so did the offensive fireworks as the Chiefs won all three games on the season-opening road trip, blasting Oakland 32–10 and Boston 43–24. Dawson tossed three touchdown passes, including two to tight end Fred Arbanas, and Garrett scored for the second consecutive week on a 42-yard run against the Raiders. Chris Burford caught ten passes for 165 yards and three touchdowns in the romp over the Patriots.

Week four would not only be the home opener for the Chiefs—it would be a rematch against the Bills. And this time the AFL's best defense did show up, stifling the Chiefs, 29–14. This time Coan rushed for only 4 yards, and Kansas City as a team rushed for only 51 yards. Can't run, can't win.

That brought an end to an eight-game winning streak by the Chiefs—the 1965 finale, the four exhibition games, and the first three games of the 1966 season. Winning was becoming a habit for these Chiefs. So was this loss an aberration . . . a blip on the screen?

There were two positives to come out of that Sunday afternoon at Municipal Stadium, one on the field and one off. On the field, Taylor caught four passes for 125 yards and a touchdown for his first 100-yard game of the season. Off the field, the fans were back. The largest crowd since the Chiefs moved to Kansas City turned out—43,885. The Chiefs averaged 20,380 per game in their first three seasons in Kansas City playing mediocre football. But the fans showed they would fill Municipal up for quality football.

Taylor followed up his Buffalo performance with a five-catch, 103-yard effort in a 37–10 throttling of the hapless Broncos the following week. But for the second time that season, the Chiefs lost at home to a team they had already beaten on the road—Oakland. Tom Flores passed for 301 yards and three touchdowns as the Raiders prevailed, 34–13. It would be the only 300-yard passing game Kansas City allowed in 1966.

Another aberration? How many aberrations is a team allowed to have during a season?

As it turns out, two.

The Chiefs would not lose again the rest of the way, posting a 7-0-1 record to claim their first Western Division title since 1962 with an AFL-best 11-3-1 mark. Taylor was one of the keys. From the Buffalo game through the end of November, he collected 100 yards receiving in six of nine games. He caught five passes for 187 yards and a touchdown in a 48–23 October victory over Houston, nine passes for 133 yards, and two touchdowns in that November tie with Boston, along with six passes for 136 yards in a road victory over the Jets. Burford also caught eight passes for 109 yards and a touchdown in New York.

Taylor and Burford finished the season tied for third in the AFL in receptions with fifty-eight apiece, and Taylor finished second in yards with 1,297. Only Hall of Famer Lance Alworth of the Chargers put up better receiving numbers than Taylor in 1966.

Coan and Garrett managed two 100-yard rushing games apiece. In the season finale, Garrett rushed for 161 yards and a touchdown in twenty-five carries to power the Chiefs to a 27–17 victory over the Chargers. He rushed for a team-leading 801 yards, and Kansas City wound up rushing for more yards than any team in professional football that season (2,274).

Unsurprisingly the Chiefs led the AFL in both yards and points, averaging 365.5 yards per game on offense and scoring 448 points—90 more than anyone else in the AFL.

But surprisingly Kansas City finished second in the league in defense with a weekly yield of only 283.6 yards per game. Robinson and fellow safety Bobby Hunt intercepted ten passes apiece, and Hurston led the team with five and a half sacks. Robinson and Willie Mitchell returned interceptions for touchdowns, Bobby Bell scored on a fumble return, and wide receiver Frank Pitts scooped up a blocked punt and raced 21 yards for another score against Boston.

And suddenly the Chiefs were one game away from becoming the first team to represent the league founded by their owner against an NFL team.

"As the season progressed it got interesting," Burford said. "The first nine to ten games it didn't really come into play. You've got to win your division, and then you have to win your championship to get there. The newspapers put more emphasis on it as we got closer to the end of the season. But we pretty much paid attention to our business. If you don't, you get your ass kicked. So we didn't spend a lot of time early in the year thinking about it."

But the Chiefs were thinking about it now.

15 The Rockpile

The AFL was trying to prove it was playing major league football, but its teams were playing in minor league stadiums.

The AFL didn't have buildings with the history of Lambeau Field, the Los Angeles Coliseum, or Yankee Stadium. It lacked buildings with the majesty of Cleveland's eighty-thousand-seat Municipal Stadium or Detroit's fifty-six-thousand-seat Briggs Stadium.

The Oakland Raiders spent their formative years playing at Frank Youell Field—capacity twenty thousand. The Boston Patriots played their first three seasons at twenty-thousand-seat Nickerson Field on the Boston University campus. The Houston Oilers spent their championship seasons at a stadium built by the city's public school system. The Denver Broncos and Kansas City Chiefs played in baseball stadiums retrofitted for football. Neither building sat thirty-five thousand.

Then there was the Rockpile.

War Memorial Stadium was built on an abandoned quarry on Buffalo's East side, thus the "Rockpile." It had been around since 1937, housing college football games, stock car races, and minor league baseball in addition to the AFL Bills. It was thirty years old in 1966 and showing its age.

The Rockpile was a home field only a home team could appreciate.

"Playing in Buffalo was kind of a tough deal," Kansas City wide receiver Chris Burford said. "It was the only stadium that you had to walk from the end zone, through the concourse, through the crowd, then go up these little steel stairs, and into this crappy little locker room. High school locker rooms were bigger. They had those little metal lockers. They had six shower heads, and you're lucky if three of them worked. It was unbelievable.

"We'd come out of our locker room, and people would be talking to you, giving you shit. You walked through the stands to get onto the field. And the field was a piece of crap. It never dried out. It was a shitty field."

Playing in Buffalo was a miserable experience for visitors, and the Bills added to that misery. Since Jack Kemp stepped into the Buffalo huddle at the tail end of the 1962 season, the Bills won almost 70 percent of their games at War Memorial Stadium, including the 1964 AFL championship against San Diego.

"It really wasn't built for football," said Bills cornerback Booker Edgerson about the Rockpile. "The locker rooms were terrible. The seating capacity was terrible. [At the] player benches, the fans were about three feet behind you. But our advantage was that it was one of the worst fields that we played on. Guys weren't used to playing on something like that. So the Rockpile may have had an impact on other teams. I don't have any great memories of the Rockpile other than the fact we won there a lot."

And it was the Rockpile that awaited the Kansas City Chiefs for the 1966 AFL championship game. But the Chiefs would have a greater concern than the stadium. Or the field. Or the tiny metal lockers.

The concern was the Bills themselves, appearing in their third consecutive championship game. Buffalo was a team that knew how to win with the players to do it. Eleven Bills were heading to the AFL All-Star Game later in January, six on offense and five on defense. Quarterback Jack Kemp, AFL Rookie of the Year Bobby Burnett, fullback Wray Carlton, tight end Paul Costa, tackle Stew Barber, and guard Billy Shaw comprised the offensive contingent, and tackle Jim Dunaway, linebackers Mike Stratton and John Tracey, cornerback Butch Byrd, and safety George Saimes comprised the defensive delegation.

It was that defense that was keeping Hank Stram up at night.

Kansas City was a run-first team. The Chiefs were the only team in the AFL that rushed for 2,000 yards that season. Stram knew he would need a ground game to win on a bad field—a January field that figured to deteriorate by the quarter with rain in the forecast.

But nobody in professional football defensed the run like the Bills with their four-man front of ends Ron McDole and Tom Day and tackles Dunaway and Tom Sestak. The Dallas Cowboys led the NFL in run defense in 1966, allowing an average of only 84 yards per game and 3.3 yards per carry. The Bills allowed an average of 75 yards per game and 3.1 yards per carry. Buffalo allowed only six rushing touchdowns all season—and two of them came against the Chiefs on the second weekend of the season.

Kansas City was the highest scoring team in the AFL with 448 points, including forty-two in that first meeting against the Bills in September. But in the rematch in Kansas City in October the Buffalo defense lopped 28 points off that total in a 29–14 victory. No one scored more than 24 points against the Bills the rest of the way as the Bills allowed the fewest points in the AFL at 255.

The Bills expected to stop the run. They had stopped it in both of their championship seasons. Their concern was Dawson, the AFL's most efficient passer that season with a 101.7 rating. He threw for twenty-six touchdowns with only ten interceptions. He was a quarterback who didn't beat himself with mistakes.

"There were quarterbacks with better arms and more talent," George Saimes said. "But what set Len apart was what he had upstairs. He had good football sense. He was very, very cool, and he was very good under pressure."

Dawson also had the best set of pass catchers of his five-year tenure as Kansas City's quarterback. Tight end Fred Arbanas and Chris Burford both played with Dawson on the 1962 championship team, but Otis Taylor gave the Chiefs a unique element that had been lacking on the flank—that combination of power and speed. Those three receivers combined to catch twenty of Dawson's twenty-six touchdown passes that season.

"Len was a perfect blend of talent into the Kansas City scheme, which was the exact opposite of (Joe) Namath," Butch Byrd said. "Namath was the team. Len had so many tools, and he used them. He was the field general behind the whole thing. Clearly Len didn't have the stats that Namath had. But he was as vital to his organization as Joe Namath or Bart Starr was to his. Len always seemed to exude confidence. He always felt he was going to win, and it carried over to the other players."

The Bills allowed a combined 7 points in the two previous AFL title games and shut out the San Diego Chargers in the 1965 game. They trusted their defense. *Defense wins championships.*

"There was no doubt in my mind we were going to win that football game," Edgerson said.

The game started off the way the Bills hoped it would: Buffalo would receive the opening kickoff, get the ball, get the lead, and then turn the game over to the defense.

Back in the 1960s there were few "specialists." The special teams were populated with starters. Lou Groza was an NFL All-Decade tackle for the Cleveland Browns in the 1950s. He also retired after the 1967 season as the NFL's all-time leading scorer with 1,608 kicking points. Yale Lary became a Hall of Fame safety for the Detroit Lions in the 1950s–60s. He also led the league in punting three times. Bobby Bell was the deep snapper with the Chiefs in addition to his duties as linebacker. Multitasking was the order of the day in the 1960s.

So it was cornerback Fletcher Smith kicking off for the Chiefs to open the championship game on a wet, frigid day at the Rockpile. His kick was short and scooped up by defensive end Dudley Meredith, who fumbled. Jerrel Wilson fell on it for the Chiefs at the Buffalo 31. Wilson, by the way, was named to the All-Time AFL team as the punter.

Three plays later, Dawson zipped a 29-yard touchdown pass to Arbanas for a 7–0 lead. But the Bills tied it later in the quarter on a 69-yard pass from Kemp to Elbert Dubenion. A 28-yard punt return by Mike Garrett early in the second quarter gave the Chiefs possession at the Buffalo 45. Six plays later Dawson threw his second 29-yard touchdown pass of the day, this time to Taylor.

But again the Bills responded, driving to the Kansas City 8 in the closing minutes of the first half. Kemp took a shot at the end zone, but safety Johnny Robinson intercepted his pass at the goal line and raced 72 yards to the Buffalo 28. Mike Mercer kicked a 32-yard field goal with three seconds left in the half to give the Chiefs a 17–7 lead.

Two mistakes by the Bills were converted into 10 points by the Chiefs, and this game was over. Garrett scored twice on the ground in the fourth quarter to close out Kansas City's stunning 31–7 victory.

"We liked being the underdogs," Bobby Bell said.

The Bills had good reason to be concerned about Dawson. He completed 16-of-24 passes for 227 yards and two touchdowns with no turnovers in miserable weather conditions. It was like he was back in high school playing against Middleton.

The talk before the game was about the Buffalo defense. The talk after the game was the Kansas City defense. The Chiefs held Buffalo's two All-Star backs Burnett and Carlton to a combined 37 rushing yards and harassed Kemp into a 12-of-27 passing performance with four sacks and two interceptions. The Bills managed only nine first downs, closing the window on their greatness. Buffalo finished 4–10 in 1967, and it would be twenty-two years before the Bills returned to another AFC championship game.

"It started off bad for us with the fumble on the opening kickoff," Edgerson said. "It was doomed from the get-go."

Kansas City would represent the AFL in the first world championship game. The Chiefs didn't know whom they would play. But the Chiefs knew whom they wanted to play.

A Dallas Showdown? 16

Pro football offered up a championship doubleheader on January 1, 1967. The AFL played the early game that day in an eastern city (Buffalo), and the NFL played the late game in a western city (Dallas).

The Kansas City Chiefs claimed the AFL title with a victory over the Bills, then had to wait to find out which NFL team they would play in the first AFL-NFL championship game, either the Dallas Cowboys or the Green Bay Packers.

The Chiefs were pulling for the Cowboys—not that Kansas City was trying to avoid Vince Lombardi and the defending NFL champion Packers. It's just that the Texans believed they had some unfinished business with the Cowboys.

The only reason the Cowboys were in existence was because of the Chiefs. Lamar Hunt founded the AFL in August 1959 and chose his hometown of Dallas to house the flagship franchise. The established NFL responded to the formation of a new, competing league by luring away the AFL ownership of the Minneapolis franchise with the promise of an expansion team in 1961 and also awarding an expansion franchise to Clint Murchison for Dallas in January 1960.

The AFL Texans and NFL Cowboys would play in the same building—the Cotton Bowl—competing for the same fans and many of the same players. For three years the two franchises flailed away at each other, miserable failures at the gate. Neither team averaged more than twenty-three thousand fans per game over the first three years in the spacious seventy-five-thousand-seat Cotton Bowl.

The Texans were the better team on the field, winning 59.5 percent of their games, punctuated by an AFL championship in 1962. The Cowboys won only nine games in three years but believed they were playing a better brand of football against superior competition than the AFL.

Hogwash, said the Texans.

"I think we'd have kicked their ass," receiver Chris Burford said. "When we were in Dallas we were hoping we could play them. They had a lot of old players on their last legs. They had some good young guys like (quarterback Don) Meredith. But I don't think they had the players we had. We would have loved to have played them, but it wasn't going to happen."

It was a frustrating situation for both franchises. A town that embraced college football and filled the Cotton Bowl on Saturdays had such a passive interest in the pro game. It didn't matter that the Texans were building a team that could win a championship or that the Cowboys were hosting games involving some of the biggest names in the sport—Jim Brown, Johnny Unitas, Bobby Layne, and Sam Huff. No one was showing up on Sundays.

"Businesses were afraid to support one team because obviously the Murchisons were a well-financed family and team," Texans owner Lamar Hunt said. "People didn't want to take sides. They would buy four tickets—four from us, four from the Cowboys—and not use any of them, just keep going to the college games."

The situation was a financial loser for both franchises. So it was the Texans who left town in 1963, conceding to the NFL a Dallas market that would not support two teams. Hunt took his team and his league to Kansas City and rebranded his franchise as the Chiefs.

"I've had a dislike for the Cowboys to this day because they stayed and we left," said offensive lineman Jerry Cornelison, an SMU product and an original Texan who started in the 1962 championship game and sixty-nine other games in his five seasons with the franchise.

Seventeen of the twenty-two starters for the 1966 Chiefs were drafted by the NFL, including first-rounders Len Dawson, Ed Budde, and Johnny Robinson. Those players didn't buy the perception that their talent level diminished because they opted to sign with the AFL instead of the NFL.

"I played in the East-West Shrine Game and the Hula Bowl, and (Don) Meredith was my quarterback," Burford said. "I caught a touchdown pass in the Shrine game from him. Now he's the quarterback for the Cowboys. So when they said you couldn't play in their league, we ignored it."

The two Dallas teams went head-to-head in the draft for several players—SMU quarterback Don Meredith in 1960, Texas Tech linebacker E. J. Holub and TCU defensive tackle Bob Lilly in 1961, Navy quarterback Roger Staubach in 1964, and Oklahoma State fullback Walt Garrison in 1966. The Texans/Chiefs landed only one of them: Holub. The Cowboys signed the other four, and two produced Pro Football Hall of Fame careers: Lilly and Staubach. Meredith and Lilly started for the Cowboys in 1966, and Holub started for the Texans.

"I played one year with Don at SMU, but once he made the decision to go with the Cowboys over the Texans, I didn't have anything more to do with him," Cornelison said. "Those guys were on the other side of town. I was more concerned about playing Earl Faison that week than what Bob Lilly was doing over at the Cowboys."

But all the Chiefs were curious how Lilly would do on January 1, 1967. Not to mention how Meredith, Lee Roy Jordan, Bob Hayes, and Chuck Howley would do. The Packers had not lost an NFL championship game since 1960. The Cowboys needed Lilly and company to bring their A game for this one. And the Chiefs were pulling for that type of performance from their old rivals.

It was a bittersweet moment for the AFL champion Chiefs—the NFL title game was being played at a sold-out Cotton Bowl, where only 18,384 showed up to see the final home game ever played by the Texans in 1962. The city of Dallas finally embraced a professional football team—and it was the Cowboys.

The old Texans wanted a little payback.

But this wasn't the same Cowboys team that the Texans left behind in Dallas in 1962. There were only five starters on the 1962 Cowboys still starting for Dallas in 1966: Lilly, Howley, defensive end George Andrie, safety Mike Gaechter, and fullback Don Perkins.

The draft board of Gil Brandt had been producing annual dividends for the Cowboys. Middle linebacker Lee Roy Jordan arrived in 1963; cornerback Mel Renfro and wide receiver Bob Hayes in 1964; halfback Dan Reeves, offensive tackle Ralph Neely, and defensive tackle Jethro Pugh in

1995; and guard John Niland and Garrison in 1966. In addition, Meredith emerged as a franchise quarterback in the four years the Texans were away and converted college basketball player Cornell Green surprisingly developed into a Pro Bowl cornerback.

Tom Landry was building momentum since the Texans left town. The Cowboys posted their first non-losing season in 1965 (7–7) and their first winning season in 1966 (10-3-1). Those ten victories gave the Cowboys the Eastern Conference championship, sending them to the NFL title game against the Packers.

In 1962 the Cowboys finished thirteenth in the fourteen-team league in defense. In 1966 the Cowboys finished second to the St. Louis Cardinals in defense. Dallas also gained the most yards and scored the most points in the NFL on offense that season. Hayes led the NFL with thirteen touchdown receptions, and the Cowboys actually had more players voted to the Pro Bowl (nine) that season than the Packers (eight).

Still, Green Bay was favored by a touchdown. But the Cowboys had the talent to play with the Packers plus the home field, where they had won nine of their last eleven games. The Cowboys and Texans both had their fingers crossed.

Then the Packers showed up. And just like in Buffalo earlier in the day, a fumbled kickoff in the first quarter proved pivotal. Green Bay converted its opening drive into a 17-yard touchdown pass from Bart Starr to Elijah Pitts for a 7–0 lead. Then Renfro fumbled the ensuing kickoff at his own 18, and rookie fullback Jim Grabowski scooped it up and took it in for a Green Bay touchdown and a 14–0 lead.

When the Dallas offense finally got onto the field, it showed why it led the NFL in explosion. The Cowboys rushed for two touchdowns—a 3-yarder by Reeves and a 23-yarder by Perkins—to tie the game by the end of the first quarter.

But Starr threw three more touchdown passes—a 51-yarder to Carroll Dale in the second quarter, a 16-yarder to Boyd Dowler in the third quarter, and a 28-yarder by Max McGee in the fourth quarter to help the Packers rebuild a 34–20 lead. But Lilly kept it a two-score game by blocking Don Chandler's extra-point kick following the McGee touchdown.

That gave the Cowboys life. On a third-and-20 from his own 32, Meredith hit Frank Clarke with a 68-yard touchdown pass, cutting the deficit to 34–27. The Dallas defense then forced a Green Bay punt—a 17-yard shank by Chandler—which set the Cowboys up at the Green Bay 47 with 2:12 remaining.

Meredith again found Clarke with a 21-yard pass, and a 4-yard run by Perkins moved the Cowboys to the Green Bay 22. A pass interference penalty against Green Bay safety Tom Brown advanced the Cowboys to the Packer 2. Over the next three snaps, Reeves rushed for a yard, dropped a pass, and offensive tackle Jim Boeke was penalized 5 yards for illegal procedure. A 4-yard pass to tight end Pettis Norman put the Cowboys back at the original line of scrimmage, the Green Bay 2.

But now it was fourth down with forty seconds remaining. The Cowboys rolled Meredith out to his right, but Green Bay linebacker Dave Robinson was quickly on him. That forced Meredith to float a pass to Hayes into the end zone where it was intercepted by Brown—and the Packers were once again NFL champions.

Maybe the Packers were predestined to win, going back almost eight years. On a frigid December day in New York, the Baltimore Colts and the New York Giants squared off in the 1958 NFL championship game. It was the first overtime game in NFL history and has long been billed as "the greatest game ever played." Lombardi was the offensive coordinator of the Giants, and Tom Landry was the defensive coordinator.

The Giants won the overtime toss, but their first possession dwindled into a fourth-and-1 situation at the New York 29. Landry told head coach Jim Lee Howell, "You've got to punt the ball." But Lombardi had a different take. "Any good team can make one yard," he told Howell. Lombardi did not want to give the ball back to Johnny Unitas. But Howell sided with Landry, and the Giants punted the football away. Unitas then drove the Colts 80 yards for the game-winning touchdown.

Lombardi never forgot, and his wife Marie said Vince always told her, "We should have gone for one . . . We should have gone for one."

"Of all the people we played against, Vince did not want to lose to Landry," Robinson said.

And Lombardi never did lose to the Cowboys as coach of the Packers, posting a 5–0 record.

So the dream of a Chiefs-Cowboys inaugural AFL/NFL championship game died on the field where it all started—the Cotton Bowl.

The Lombardi Packers 17

Losing was not part of Vince Lombardi's DNA. He can thank Jack Vainisi for that.

Hall of Famers Don Hutson, Tony Canadeo, and Curly Lambeau were long gone from Green Bay's championship era of the 1930s and 1940s when the Packers hired Vainisi as their director of player personnel in 1950. Green Bay had fallen on hard times and, coming off a 2–10 season, were desperate enough to hire a twenty-three-year-old to restock their roster.

And what a restock Vainisi engineered. He conducted Green Bay's drafts for eleven years before passing away in November 1960 of a heart attack at the age of thirty-three. But his thumbprints were all over Lombardi's success in the 1960s. Vainisi gave Lombardi the pieces he would need to win those five championships that decade.

Vainisi drafted twenty-two players who went to Pro Bowls for the Packers and three other players who went to Pro Bowls for other teams. His draft picks went to a combined seventy-three Pro Bowls. He also drafted eight Hall of Famers, including three in consecutive rounds of the 1958 draft: Jim Taylor, Ray Nitschke, and Jerry Kramer.

Vainisi drafted three players who would become NFL MVPs in the 1960s: Paul Hornung, Jim Taylor, and Bart Starr. One of his draft choices was named to the NFL's one-hundredth-anniversary team (Forrest Gregg), another was named to the NFL's seventy-fifth-anniversary team (Nitschke), and four more were named to the NFL's fiftieth-anniversary team (Herb Adderley, Boyd Dowler, Jerry Kramer, and Ron Kramer).

Vainisi drafted end Billy Howton, who retired in 1963 as the NFL's all-time leading receiver. He drafted Tobin Rote, who won an NFL passing title with the Packers and went on to quarterback the Detroit Lions to an

NFL championship and the San Diego Chargers to an AFL title. Vainisi also was the driving force behind Green Bay's hiring of Lombardi in 1959 after eleven consecutive losing seasons.

Lombardi proved to be the final piece of Vainisi's championship equation. Lombardi informed his squad from the start that losing was not an option and then drove them mentally and physically into acceptance of his credo.

"The influence Lombardi had on that team—and the demands he placed on that team—were unbelievable," said Paul Wiggin, a Pro Bowl defensive end with the Cleveland Browns. "You're on the field, and you can hear that bellowing Eastern accent. You talk about shattering. Not only when he was screaming at his players on the field, but it was demoralizing you on defense. You talk about [speaking] with authority. That's command as I've never seen it."

Max McGee, Bob Skoronski, Gregg, Starr, Ron Kramer, Hornung, Taylor, Nitschke, and Jerry Kramer all arrived in Green Bay in the 1950s and were members of the 1958 team that won just one game. The talent was underachieving in Green Bay. Then Lombardi arrived. All nine of those players would start on championship teams in the 1960s, and all would go to their first Pro Bowls under Lombardi.

A 17th-round draft pick in 1956, Starr floundered in his first three NFL seasons, starting only nineteen of Green Bay's thirty-six games and throwing almost twice as many interceptions (twenty-five) as touchdowns (thirteen). He won only three of his starts, and his career track seemed to be on a bullet train to Canada. Even the arrival of Lombardi wasn't enough to resurrect Starr's career. Not at first, anyway.

Lombardi acquired Lamar McHan in a trade with the Chicago Cardinals in May of 1959. He was the second overall choice of the 1954 draft with five years of NFL starting experience. So McHan walked into Lombardi's first lineup. He won his first three starts, all at home, before the Los Angeles Rams came to town and blasted the Packers, 45–6. Green Bay then hit the road for a three-game trip to Baltimore, New York, and Chicago and lost all three. The Bears knocked McHan out of the game with a leg injury, and it was now Starr's turn.

Starr completed only 14-of-40 passes with three interceptions against the defending NFL champion Colts for another loss. Then he closed the season by winning his last four starts to give Lombardi a successful season (7–5) in his head-coaching debut. Starr threw only one interception in winning his last three starts, all on the road against Detroit, Los Angeles, and San Francisco.

Lombardi was one of the "Seven Blocks of Granite" that formed the offensive line at Fordham in the 1930s. True to his blocking roots, Lombardi was a run-first head coach. He needed a quarterback who could make plays when the Packers needed them to be made. Lombardi wasn't asking his quarterback to win games. He was asking him not to lose them. In doing so, he was maximizing Starr.

The Cleveland Browns made Henry Jordan a fifth-round draft choice in 1957 but had little use for him. He spent his first twenty-four games in the NFL as a backup with very little statistically to show for his career. Lombardi traded a fourth-round draft pick for Jordan in 1959 and plugged him into the starting lineup as a defensive tackle. The Packers improved from 11th in the NFL in run defense without Jordan to seventh with him, shaving 23 yards per game off their average. Lombardi was maximizing Jordan.

A year later Lombardi made another trade with the Browns for another backup defensive lineman, Willie Davis. Lombardi plugged him in at left defensive end, and Davis sacked six quarterbacks in 1960. Lombardi was maximizing Davis.

"Vince wanted each of us to play to his maximum potential," Taylor said. "Hornung had his limitations. Bart the same way. Jerry Kramer, Fuzzy Thurston, Willie Davis, Herb Adderley . . . we all in our own right had a certain amount of ability, and we played to our potential game-in and game-out."

Taylor was a bruising fullback at LSU in the same 1957 backfield as Billy Cannon and Johnny Robinson. He averaged 4.7 yards per carry for the Tigers and scored a team-leading twelve touchdowns. Green Bay invested a second-round draft pick in Taylor in 1958 but then didn't use him. He started only two games and carried the ball just fifty-two times with one touchdown.

Enter Lombardi and the emergence of Taylor as a force. Lombardi doubled his workload and tripled his starts in 1959. A year later Taylor would lead the NFL with his 230 carries. Lombardi maximized Taylor.

"I was never concerned about yardage when I played football," Taylor said. "I tried to be the best running back for the Green Bay Packers that day, game-in and game-out. I never asked myself, 'Did I get 100 yards today?' I remember a game we played against the Giants or Bears in Milwaukee, and I gained 140 or 160 yards and scored three touchdowns. But that next Tuesday I was getting my fanny chewed for missing a red-dog blitz. Statistics-wise, I did fine, but I wasn't a complete player that day."

Former UCLA coach Red Sanders coined the phrase, "Winning isn't everything—it's the only thing." It was a phrase Lombardi repeated to his players because he believed it. During his stay with the Packers, Lombardi coached 122 regular season games and won eighty-nine of them with four others ending in a tie. He coached ten playoff games and won nine of them. When it mattered most, Lombardi won. Even when it didn't matter. Lombardi coached fifty exhibition games with the Packers and won forty-two of them.

"I remember Fuzz (fellow guard Thurston) and I played an entire exhibition season without getting a play off," Jerry Kramer said. "We looked at one another, shrugged our shoulders, and said, 'Well, that's the way it is.' He believed you prepared yourself to play properly by playing properly. He wanted to win every time he stepped on the field."

Green Bay vaulted from last to third in the Western Conference with that 7–5 record in Lombardi's debut season. The next year the Packers won the West and reached the NFL championship game but fell just yards and seconds short of victory. The clock expired with the Packers at the Philadelphia 9-yard line, allowing the Eagles to escape with a 17–13 victory.

"The feeling was we didn't lose games, time just ran out on us," Davis said. "Lombardi made it so difficult for you to accept defeat. So it couldn't be administered. You refused to accept defeat. It seems rather difficult for someone that's never been there, but I think we built this sense of . . . hey, we cannot accept defeat. There are very few ties. You either win or lose. Winning, as Lombardi used to say, is a habit that becomes a natural thing to do. He convinced us that winning was the natural thing for us to expect. In many ways I felt we probably experienced that more than any team in the NFL."

Lombardi wasn't Hank Stram. He wasn't relying on motion, reverses, and trickery on offense. He relied on basic, fundamental football: Drill your players to do the same thing over and over again. Be better than the guy across the line from you. Repetitious behavior became the key to success.

"The Packers had only about six plays," said Detroit Hall of Fame cornerback Dick LeBeau. "There were variations of them. The challenge was to stop them."

The power sweep was the staple of the Lombardi playbook with guards Kramer and Thurston pulling and Taylor leading Hornung around end. Until a defense proved it could stop the sweep, the Packers were going to run it over and over again. Lombardi was less worried about his opponent than he was his own team. Do enough things right on Sunday and you'll win regardless of whom you're playing.

"Our plays and our focus on the game didn't change much in the nine years Lombardi was there," Jerry Kramer said. "We occasionally made adjustments for certain players like Deacon Jones. He was a great pass rusher with great quickness. So we put the tight end up there right next to Forrest, and it neutralized Deacon. Sometimes we'd run at this guy a little bit to keep him honest. But very seldom did we make any significant changes. We just went with what we had."

That loss to the Eagles did not devastate the Packers. Far from it. Green Bay returned to the NFL championship game again in 1961—as well as 1962 and 1965, winning each time.

"We knew how to win," Davis said. "I think the edge would have been in the attitude and the confidence, believing that we could win even when things didn't go well. It wasn't a case of being the physically superior team as it was just knowing how to win. You knew how to play. We were winning as a team then. Lombardi had spent all those years preparing us how to win."

And as the first team representing the NFL in the inaugural AFL-NFL championship game, the Packers expected to win.

A Fear of the Unknown 18

The Green Bay Packers knew what to expect when they faced the Philadelphia Eagles in the first championship game of the Vince Lombardi era in 1960.

There was a way of measuring the Eagles. The Packers had game film from their 1958 meeting with the Eagles, plus film of Philadelphia games against the Dallas Cowboys, Detroit Lions, and Pittsburgh Steelers in 1960. All were common opponents of the Packers that season. Green Bay could gauge the arm strength of Philadelphia quarterback Norm Van Brocklin, the speed of end Pete Retzlaff, and the range of linebacker Chuck Bednarik.

Green Bay knew what to expect when the Packers faced the New York Giants in both the 1961 and 1962 championship games. They knew what to expect from the Cleveland Browns in 1965 and the Dallas Cowboys in 1966 in those championship games. The Packers had the game films of the common opponents, so they had a feel for the ability of the players and the relative strengths and weaknesses of each team.

But the Packers had no idea what to expect from the Kansas City Chiefs in the first AFL-NFL championship game in 1967. There were no game films against common opponents. Just Kansas City game films against Buffalo, Denver, and Houston—cities and teams foreign to the NFL.

"We didn't know anything about them other than what you could see on film," Green Bay offensive tackle Forrest Gregg said. "You had a hard time evaluating them because you didn't know how good the competition was. The uncertainty of what you were facing was as tough as anything else. You didn't want to undersell them. On the other hand, you didn't want to oversell them from a standpoint of having some fear of them."

The Packers didn't necessarily fear the Chiefs as much as they may have feared the unknown. And that was real.

"I was nervous in the first championship (1961) in Green Bay," defensive end Willie Davis said. "But Lombardi always talked about winning—'*We were not going to be whipped in Lambeau Field on this day by anybody.*' In that sense, I think I was nervous, but nervous in the right way. There was almost a sense of how well you were going to play.

"But in that first Super Bowl, I was nervous on the basis of, 'Oh my God, what happens if these guys somehow get a monster by the tail and we become the laughing stock of the NFL and pro football?' That added another dimension of fear."

But the more film the Packers viewed of the Chiefs, the more confident they became.

"I remember watching films one evening, and two of the Kansas City safeties ran into each other, and both fell down," Jerry Kramer said. "It was very unusual. Max (McGee) said, 'Run that back—watch these safeties.' And they rewind the film, run it back, and Max started humming the Looney Tunes and Merry Melody theme as if it's a comedy."

McGee could afford to be a clown. He wasn't expected to play in the Super Bowl, having caught only ten passes all season sitting behind Pro Bowl wide receivers Carroll Dale and Boyd Dowler. But the rest of the Packers were searching for a smidgen of common ground—a smidgen of familiarity with the Chiefs. They found it in quarterback Len Dawson.

One Packer, defensive tackle Henry Jordan, played on the same NFL field as Dawson. As a backup quarterback for the Steelers, Dawson threw three passes in mop-up duty against Jordan's Cleveland Browns in 1958. Dawson spent five seasons in the NFL but started only one game and threw only forty-five career passes before escaping to the AFL in 1962.

"We knew he was a castoff," cornerback Herb Adderley said, "and we observed that his height might have been an issue. We played better quarterbacks than Dawson. Johnny Unitas was the best I ever played against. (Bart) Starr and Unitas were the only two quarterbacks I know that could call an entire game at the line of scrimmage. But we respected Dawson. Lombardi wouldn't have it any other way."

Kansas City shared Green Bay's uncertainty. The Chiefs knew of Lombardi and all the championships. But this wasn't the same team. Eleven starters remained in 1966 from the 1961 team that won the first championship. Starr, Taylor, Dowler, Gregg, Skoronski, Kramer, Thurston, Davis, Jordan, Nitschke, and Wood were all in their twenties then. Except for Dowler (twenty-nine), all were now in their thirties. Young legs were dynamic legs. Older legs relied on experience.

This time around the Chiefs had the young, dynamic legs. At thirty-one, Dawson was the only player in the Kansas City starting lineup in his thirties. The average age of the Kansas City starting lineup was 26.8. When the Chiefs looked at the Packers, did they see a championship-caliber team or an aging team whose dynasty was running on fumes?

"We didn't know," running back Mike Garrett said. "We watched them play, and when they played good teams, they played well. But we knew some of the teams in the NFL weren't as good as we were. So it was a big question when we got there. Just what would happen?"

The NFL Pro Bowl was to be played the following week in the Los Angeles Coliseum, and the players were to report the day of the Super Bowl. As a perk, the Pro Bowlers were given 50-yard-line seats for the game. There was one NFLer who thought the Chiefs had a chance—rookie linebacker Tommy Nobis, the first overall choice in both the AFL and NFL drafts who spurned his home state Houston Oilers to sign with the Atlanta Falcons.

"By the time I came into the league, the AFL had already proven themselves," Nobis said. "The Chiefs had outstanding talent. If it had been another team, I might not have felt that way. But the Kansas City Chiefs during that era were outstanding. How many guys off that Kansas City team are in the Hall of Fame now? I thought the AFL had a shot."

But Nobis was one of the few. The Packers were installed as 14-point favorites in the game.

Miller Farr played cornerback for the San Diego Chargers and earned a spot on the AFL's All-Time Team. His younger brother Mel became the NFL Rookie of the Year with the Detroit Lions in 1967. Miller played against Kansas City and knew the Chiefs. He wasn't a believer.

"I didn't think the Chiefs had a chance," Farr said. "We were hoping that the game would be close, but I didn't think they could win. Green Bay was a little better at quarterback. They had All-Pro cornerbacks, linebackers. They were awesome that year."

Dawson himself wasn't in awe of the Packers. This wasn't Green Bay's 1962 team—Lombardi's best team—that bludgeoned everyone along the way in a 14–1 championship season. The departures from the lineup of Paul Hornung (injury) and Jim Ringo (trade) left the 1966 Packers two Hall of Famers short of that 1962 team. But the Packer mystique remained.

"These were people that I had seen," Dawson said. "I was in the NFL. I had watched them when I was at Cleveland. Everyone was saying, 'The NFL can't beat these people—why do you think you can?' It was as if they were saying, 'The real guys can't do it. The real football players. What makes you think you castoffs, who aren't good enough to play in the National Football League, can do it?'

"But we had guys like (Fred) Arbanas and (Ed) Budde who had played on those great teams at Michigan State. They said, 'Hey, wait a minute. We played with those guys. Just because they put on an NFL jersey doesn't mean they're better than us."

Johnny Robinson wasn't in awe of the Packers either. He was a college teammate of one of Green Bay's best players, Jim Taylor. Robinson was the third overall pick of the 1960 NFL draft, and had he played with his drafting team, the Detroit Lions, he would have been lining up against the Packers twice a season for the past seven years.

"There was an apprehension about playing the National Football League's best team," Robinson said. "I think Green Bay at that time was one of the truly great football teams. Anybody would have some apprehension about playing them for the first time.

"But we weren't worried too much about anything. Going into the game, they didn't do anything unusual that we didn't feel we could stop. We were worried about their running attack. They just had a magnificent offensive line, tremendous personnel. A great fullback, a great quarterback, and good solid receivers. But any kind of an unknown factor is a psychological disadvantage. That hurt us, working to Green Bay's advantage rather than ours."

But there were a few Chiefs who knew the Packers were beatable.

The College All-Star Game 19

The Chicago Tribune Charities sponsored the annual College All-Star Game from 1934–76.

It was a novel concept for an exhibition football game—pick the best college players from the previous season and pit them in a game against the reigning NFL champion. How would the amateurs fare against the pros? The game was played at Soldier Field in August as a prelude to the upcoming NFL season.

Back in the 1930s the better football was played on Saturdays, not Sundays. The college team lost only one of the first five All-Star Games in the 1930s, then won three more times during the World War II years. But by the time the 1950s rolled around, the NFL was in command. From 1948–62, the NFL champions posted a 12–3 record with the Philadelphia Eagles (1950), Cleveland Browns (1955), and Detroit Lions (1958) the only losers.

In 1962 Vince Lombardi took Green Bay to his first All-Star Game, and the Packers trounced the collegians, 42–20, to improve the NFL's overall record to 19-8-2. Green Bay was an offensive juggernaut with future Hall of Famers Bart Starr, Jim Taylor, and Paul Hornung in the backfield. Starr, in fact, threw five touchdown passes in that game. The only other NFL team in the history of the series to reach 40 points against the All-Stars was the 1940 Packers with Hall of Famers Curly Lambeau as their coach and Don Hutson as their star performer.

The Packers were the best team in the NFL again in 1962—in fact, the best team of the Lombardi era. Green Bay scored the most points in the NFL that season (415) and allowed the fewest (148). The Packers pranced through the regular season with a 13–1 record, then traveled to New York and whipped the Giants, 16–7, in the championship game.

The Packers returned to the College All-Star Game in 1963 with all nine of their Pro Bowlers back from the previous season. The only lineup absence was their golden boy Hornung, who, along with Detroit defensive tackle Alex Karras, had been suspended by NFL commissioner Pete Rozelle for the 1963 season for gambling. But with Starr and 1962 NFL MVP Taylor returning, the Packers still had the weaponry to squash the All-Stars.

Except that they didn't.

Remember, Lombardi didn't like losing to anyone, anywhere, any time. Much less a bunch of collegians. But the All-Stars rode the arm of Wisconsin quarterback Ron Vander Kelen to a 20–17 victory, ending Lombardi's streak of nineteen consecutive exhibition victories. The last time Lombardi lost an August game was in 1959 during his first season with the Packers.

There were three other notable players on the 1963 All-Star team—Bobby Bell, Buck Buchanan, and Ed Budde. All had been drafted by the defending AFL champion Dallas Texans, and all started that night against the Packers. Budde, in fact, was a captain of the All-Star team.

"We ate Green Bay alive," Bell said. "They couldn't do anything. We were all seniors in college, and we kicked their butts. People couldn't believe it. Vince Lombardi said he was totally embarrassed having some college guys come in here and whip our butts."

The College All-Star Game changed the career track of Bell. He played offensive tackle and defensive end at the University of Minnesota, winning the Outland Trophy as the nation's best lineman. But All-Star coach Otto Graham was not impressed with what he saw from Bell on the practice field.

"He called Coach Stram and told him, 'You wasted your money. Bobby Bell can't play,'" Bell said. "He wouldn't play me at offensive tackle or defensive end. He told me to go to the other end of the field and work with the linebackers. I said I'd never done that, and he said, 'Go down there. You can't stay up here.'"

Like Bell, Dave Robinson was a two-way player at Penn State, earning All-American honors at tight end and also playing end on defense. After brief trials at both tight end and defensive end in the All-Star camp, Robinson received the same treatment from Graham, who told him he too should go down to the other end of the field and work with the linebackers. Robinson even wore the number in the All-Star Game that he was assigned as a tight end: 86.

"We had no idea what we were doing," Bell said.

But that August night against the world champion Packers, Bell and Robinson both made their first-ever starts at linebacker. Both players now have busts in the Pro Football Hall of Fame for their play at the position.

Graham also started Buck Buchanan at defensive tackle. But not without some encouragement.

"One day [Graham] read off the starting lineup," Robinson said. "He didn't want to play Buck. But Buck threatened him. I think Buck was halfway kidding. But the next time they announced the starting lineup, Buck was in there."

The Rose Bowl hero Vander Kelen was the game MVP, completing 9-of-11 passes for 141 yards. A 73-yard chunk of that came in the fourth quarter on what would be the deciding touchdown of the game—a pass reception by his Wisconsin college teammate Pat Richter.

The postgame celebration didn't last long for Robinson, Ole Miss cornerback Charles Morris, and TCU offensive tackle Tony Liscio. All three had been drafted by the Packers—Robinson in the first round, Liscio in the third, and Morris in the fifth. All were invited by the Packers to the postgame buffet at the Green Bay hotel.

"The three of us walked in together, right up to Vince Lombardi," Robinson said. "He took one look at us and went, 'Hurmph . . .' and walked away. That was it. All the players didn't want to see us because they knew it was going to be a hard week of practice after losing that game—and they were blaming us! We told them, 'Hey, don't look at us. You're the guys who messed up.'"

Back in Green Bay, Lombardi was still irritated and made the entire team watch the game film together so he could critique both sides of the ball.

"Finally he got to a play that came my way," Robinson said. "I jammed (tight end) Ron Kramer and threw him off. Tom Moore was the halfback, and I dropped him to his knees. Then I made the tackle on Jim Taylor. Vince stopped the camera, and I kind of puffed my chest out. Then Vince said, 'Look at that! Look at that! Kramer . . . that kid there is a rookie, and he just beat you. He probably won't even make the team that drafted him.' And I thought, 'Oh, no . . .' My wife was home pregnant with twins. Willie Wood leaned over to me and said, 'Dave, I think he means don't buy a house in town.'"

Robinson did make his team and did buy a house in Green Bay. He also became a starter for the Packers midway through his rookie season. And he discovered that Lombardi did have a grudging respect for the 1963 College All-Star team.

"Vince told me if he could keep that All-Star team together, he'd win a world championship within three years," Robinson said.

It was also the first time African American players played prominent roles for the College All-Stars with Bell, Buchanan, Robinson, Syracuse tight end John Mackey, Nebraska fullback Bill "Thunder" Thornton, and UCLA safety Kermit Alexander leading the way.

"Jim Brown, Leroy Kelly, and Bobby Mitchell were all College All-Stars, but they never got to play," Bell said. "They all told me they were tickled to death that we won, that we beat the crap out of the Packers, because they didn't get to play. We did."

Bell, Buchanan, and Budde found another appreciative fan when they reported to camp with the Chiefs the following week. LSU teammates Johnny Robinson and Billy Cannon were two of the best players in college football in 1959. But both were barred from playing in the 1960 College All-Star Game because they had signed with the AFL. So Robinson appreciated the lick his three new teammates put on the Packers and the NFL.

Bell, Buchanan, and Budde all earned a valuable lesson that night: the Green Bay Packers were beatable.

"We looked up to those guys," Bell said. "They were NFL players. They were great. But they put their pants on the same way that we do."

Just as they would in the first AFL-NFL championship game.

Otis Taylor

20

The Kansas City Chiefs (and the AFL in general) offered African American players both a home and a voice.

Abner Haynes, Curtis McClinton, Buck Buchanan, Bobby Bell, Dave Grayson, and Mack Lee Hill were among the African American athletes welcomed with open arms in a color-blind Kansas City market. They were free to express themselves on and off the field.

But few of the Chiefs expressed themselves like wide receiver Otis Taylor. He was the big-play element for Prairie View A&M's 1963 team that became the first HBCU school ever invited to participate in the NAIA playoffs. The Panthers posted a combined 19–1 record in Taylor's final two seasons and were twice crowned the Black college national champion by Bill Nunn at the Pittsburgh Courier.

The Chiefs drafted Taylor in the fourth round in 1965 after smuggling him out of a Houston hotel under the watchful eyes of his NFL babysitters on the eve of the AFL draft.

Taylor was freaky in both size (six-three, 215 pounds) and speed (4.5 40-yard dash). Men his size weren't supposed to be that fast. But Taylor was only a bit player for the Chiefs as a rookie, playing behind veterans Chris Burford and Frank Jackson. He didn't suit up until week three and didn't start until week eleven when Burford vacated the lineup with an injury.

Taylor caught two passes for 27 yards in his first AFL start against Boston, as quarterback Len Dawson was getting comfortable throwing for the first time in his AFL career to a speed merchant. Taylor then scored a touchdown in each of his next three starts to close the season, catching 74 yards in passes in week twelve against Houston, 85 yards in passes in week thirteen against Buffalo, and 110 more in week fourteen against Denver to claim permanent possession of a starting position.

The following season, Taylor was one of the best receivers in all of football, catching fifty-eight passes for 1,297 yards—a staggering 22.4-yard average—with eight touchdowns. As his game grew, so did his voice.

There's an iconic photo of Taylor on the Kansas City bench drawing up a play in the dirt for Dawson. But it was more than a photo. It was a prognostication.

In one of Hank Stram's unique formations—and there were many—his flanker Taylor was lined up in the offensive backfield between the guard and tackle. Taylor noticed how the Bills defended that alignment, and his eyes lit up. That's when he grabbed Dawson on the sideline and drew up the play.

"Otis told me, 'When I get in that formation, Butch Byrd's got to cover me man-to-man . . . and he can't do it. He can't cover me,'" Dawson said. "That's the thing I liked about a quarterback calling his own plays. You could go to the people involved. I said, 'When do you think you can run it?' He said, 'Whenever you think is best.' So I said, 'As soon as we get the damn ball back.'

"So the first play I threw it. The wind was swirling, and I thought I overthrew him by 10 yards. I had a great release and a tight spiral. But Otis put on the afterburners and caught up with it. He fought his way down to the 8-yard line, then the next play I hit Gloster Richardson for a touchdown. That was the game."

Taylor did not limit his voice to Sundays. He voiced his opinions during the week as well. But they often weren't as well received as his sideline conversation with Dawson. One moment in particular stood out—a confrontation with his head coach Hank Stram on the practice field.

"I was acting up a little bit, having some fun," Taylor said. "I'd go up for a pass, and when I was coming down, I'd spin and catch it behind my back. Hank was standing up in his tower, and he'd holler down for me to catch the ball right. I'd say, 'It may come up in a game someday. If I need it, at least I'll have a little practice doing it.'"

Stram shouted down, "That will cost you $500, Otis."

"So I said, 'I'm through. I'm going in,'" said Taylor, abruptly leaving practice. "Looking back, it wasn't the right thing to do. But I was upset. I went home that night and prepared myself for the things I wanted to say to the man. I was going in there fired up. I was going to let him have it. I was ready."

Taylor showed up early the next day for practice and went directly to Stram's office.

"When I got there, Hank was cool and calm and acted like it never happened," Taylor said. "He had a little basket of cookies for you. He'd give you a hug and ask, 'How's Mom? How's the family . . . your father, your wife, whatever . . . he told me his wife said hello. He'd tell me that his kids asked him to say hello to 'O' for them.

"When we finished our talk, I didn't feel I had lost but did feel that he had won. He had me admitting I was wrong and that I shouldn't have done what I did. He gave me a little hug, told me to forget about the fine but asked me to 'keep it between the two of us.'"

Taylor was too important a player for the Chiefs not to afford preferential treatment. And in the lead-up to the first AFL-NFL championship game, the Packers were preparing to give Taylor special treatment as well.

"We thought they would have to go to Otis Taylor in order to beat us," said Hall of Fame cornerback Herb Adderley. "Taylor would have to come up with a big day, he and Dawson. Watching the film, I knew Otis Taylor was one of the best wide receivers in the game. But seeing the guy play on the film and seeing him in person are two different things. Otis was quicker, faster, and bigger than I thought. He was as good a receiver as any I covered. He was like (Washington Hall of Famer) Charley Taylor. Shutting down Otis Taylor was very important to the Packers."

That would be easier said than done. Taylor in the 1960s was what Hall of Famer Calvin Johnson would be for the Detroit Lions in the 2010s. Double—and even triple—coverage often didn't matter. When the ball was in the air, Taylor went and got it. When in doubt, just throw it at Otis.

Dawson remembered another game against the Patriots: "We're down deep in their end, but I couldn't find anyone so I threw the ball low and out of bounds (near the flag) just to stop the clock," Dawson said. "Well, Otis is standing over there with his toes [on the end zone] sideline. He sticks his left hand out and catches it with one hand for a touchdown. Here I'm trying to throw the darn thing out of bounds, and he catches it for a touchdown. I never said a word. After the game I told reporters, 'That was the only place I could throw it because of the defense.'"

Taylor would be a handful for Adderley and the Packers. The Chiefs ran the ball to set up the pass. They averaged 5.2 yards per carry during the regular season—a full yard more than anyone else—with an AFL-high nineteen touchdowns. If you couldn't stop a Kansas City run, it wouldn't matter how well a defense covered Taylor. The Chiefs finished 11-2-1 with Dawson throwing seventeen passes or fewer in half of the games. But if a defense loaded up to stop the run, leaving itself short in the secondary, Taylor exploded. He caught touchdown passes of 89, 77, 74, and 71 yards that season. His eight touchdowns that season averaged 52.3 yards.

"I used to get off the bench to watch Otis play," defensive tackle Buck Buchanan said. "He is without a doubt the greatest receiver I have ever seen. It was big play after big play after big play with him. What a player he was."

Mike Garrett would be another issue for the Packers. He finished as the runnerup to Buffalo's Bobby Burnett for AFL Rookie of the Year honors. Garrett rushed for 801 yards, averaging 5.5 yards per carry. McClinton added 540 yards, and Bert Coan added 521. And then there was Taylor, whom Stram liked to utilize on end-arounds. He carried the ball twice for 33 yards during the regular season. That accentuated another aspect of his game—his physicality.

"Otis loved to run with the ball," Dawson said. "In those days, receivers got pounded on. They had the bump-and-run, and those [defensive backs] were hitting you in the face, in the throat, all over. You took a physical beating, much more than they do today. So when Otis had the opportunity to give it back, he went looking for folks to deliver a shot."

The game plan would be a familiar one for the Chiefs: Play-action, play-action, play-action. Run the ball and then fake the run. Slow down the pass rush and then get Dawson out of the pocket.

"They had three great players over there on the left side—(end Willie) Davis, (linebacker Dave) Robinson, and Adderley," Dawson said. "At that time Robinson was 240. He was huge for a linebacker. We wanted to stay away from him. That's why we rolled, because when Davis was inside we could crack back on him. Nobody could block him. We had another problem with Henry Jordan on the other side, a really quick defensive lineman. He gave you fits. We knew we couldn't sit back in the pocket because we couldn't handle those people play after play."

If the Chiefs could get Dawson out of the pocket, they liked their chances for an upset. That came from film study. The Minnesota Vikings won only four games in 1966, but one of them came against the Packers in Green Bay when another short (six-foot) quarterback, Fran Tarkenton, tormented them with his legs. The best way to beat a Green Bay pass rush that featured a pair of Hall of Famers was to run away from it.

"Our defense worked best when we had containment of the quarterback," Davis said. "That was the Fran Tarkenton effect. We had learned that they hurt us more consistently when he got outside the pocket. I'm sure the Chiefs took that into consideration. We knew we'd have a helluva time if Dawson was floating."

Dawson on the move also would give him better sight lines. And Stram had another wrinkle for the Packers. The Chiefs were coming to expect weekly wrinkles from Stram.

"We always knew that once we got into a game, no one would outcoach us or outmaneuver us," Garrett said. "Hank was very good at that."

Stram's twist for the Packers was another film-study gem. He knew how effective the Green Bay linebackers were in pass coverage. All were tall and agile. All three stood six-three or taller and would drop into zone coverage in obvious passing situations, forcing the quarterback to throw the ball over their heads where the secondary would have a four-to-three edge in bodies—four defensive backs versus two wide receivers and a tight end. The trio of Ray Nitschke, Robinson, and Lee Roy Caffey intercepted ten passes that season, including five by Robinson.

The twist? The Kansas City running backs would become primary receivers in the championship game. McClinton caught only nineteen passes all season, Coan eighteen, and Garrett fifteen, but they would have ample opportunities coming out of the backfield against the Packers. Their involvement as safety valve receivers would force the Green Bay linebackers to come up in man coverage, creating wider passing lanes down the field. Dawson would have five potential targets instead of three.

"We felt we could move the ball on the Packers," Stram said, "but we didn't know if we could stop them."

And that was a legitimate concern. Although Kansas City had some great players on defense in Buchanan, Bell, Holub, Mays, and Johnny Robinson, there were some obvious soft spots.

The Chiefs had three players in the starting defensive backfield who entered professional football as free agents: cornerbacks Willie Mitchell and Fred Williamson and safety Bobby Hunt. The Chiefs also lost starting defensive tackle Ed Lothamer midway through the season with an injury. That took a six-five, 270-pound chunk out of the middle of their run defense. Lothamer was replaced by an undrafted rookie free agent, Andy Rice.

The Packers were seasoned. The Chiefs were not. Green Bay had twelve starters who had played in all four of the NFL championship games under Lombardi, and all of them had played in Pro Bowls. The average age of the Green Bay starting lineup was 28.6 years—a full two years older than the Kansas City lineup.

The Chiefs may have been young but they were big.

"You looked at the Chiefs and they were clearly a team full of recognizable names from the college circles of three and four and five years past," Davis said. "There was a lot of discussion about their size. I don't think we played against anybody in the NFL that big from end to end on offense. They were huge."

Merlin Olsen was one of the best defensive tackles in the NFL in 1966, a future Hall of Famer. He was six-five and 270 pounds. The Chiefs lined up one of the best defensive tackles in the AFL, Buck Buchanan. He was six-seven and played close to 290. Green Bay's own Forrest Gregg was the preeminent right tackle in the NFL at the time. He went six-four and 250 pounds. The Chiefs lined up Dave Hill at right tackle. He was listed at six-five and 260 pounds. Kansas City's left tackle, Jim Tyrer, was even bigger at six-six and 280 pounds.

"When I walked out there, I thought Dave Hill was one of the biggest guys I'd ever seen," Davis said. "He was like a long, tall tree. In most cases I had an eye-to-eye relationship when I looked straight ahead (at the offensive tackle). But when I looked at Hill . . . the only other player I remembered like that was (six-nine San Francisco right tackle) Bob St. Clair. You clearly had a sense of looking up at the guy.

"My first reaction was, I've got to beat this guy with speed and quickness because I won't be able to push or overpower him back to the quarterback. I saw that in films. What I didn't realize was how it seemed to be amplified when I was there on the field, and all at once I'm standing in front of him. Perception and reality come together then. My first reaction was surprise. Even though tackles (in the NFL) were starting to get bigger, especially the right tackles like Bob Brown in that six-five, six-six, six-seven range. But Hill was clearly more awesome looking than even I anticipated."

Kansas City had size and talent. But Dave Robinson could identify the Achilles heel in Green Bay's film study.

"They had excellent personnel, good ball players," Robinson said. "But when you watched them on film, their techniques were horrible. When you're supposed to come off your left foot to make a block, they'd come off with their right foot. But the competition was so weak in the AFL, they crushed them anyway."

Lombardi noticed that deficiency too.

"They were playing the Jets," Robinson said. "Their center snapped the ball, and the middle linebacker didn't move. He was looking to see which way to go, and the center just leap-frogged out, diving at the middle linebacker's ankles, and cut him down like a weed. The play was off tackle, and of course the middle linebacker is laying on the ground.

"Lombardi said, 'Stop the film! Run it back!' And they run it back, and he says, 'Nitschke, did you see that? If that guy blocks you one time on Sunday, I'm going to come out onto the field and put my foot in your rear end.' The Chiefs were so good in the AFL they didn't have to worry about technique. They could just overpower people. But when you play against the Green Bay Packers, you had to have your techniques down. That's all there was to it. They didn't have a shot in the world against us."

The Green Bay game plan was also very familiar. It was the same plan the Packers used in winning championships in 1961, 1962, and 1965. Even without Hornung, who only started six games in 1966 because of a pinched nerve in his neck and would not suit up for the Super Bowl, the Packers would run the ball. Elijah Pitts proved to be an adequate complement to the workhorse Taylor, rushing for a team-leading seven touchdowns that season.

In addition, the Packers had already drafted the heir apparents for Hornung and Taylor. Rookies Donny Anderson of Texas Tech and Jim Grabowski of Illinois were dubbed "The Gold Dust Twins," and they spent their rookie seasons in 1966 waiting their turn. The three consensus All-American running backs in 1965 would all be on the field for this game—Anderson, Grabowski, and the Heisman Trophy-winning Garrett.

The other area of concern for the Chiefs was Bart Starr, who was named the NFL MVP in 1966 when he threw a career-low three interceptions. His 105.0 passer efficiency rating won him his second NFL passing title—and he was coming off a four-touchdown pass game against the Cowboys in the NFL championship.

Both teams could see a path to victory. The Chiefs certainly didn't believe they were overmatched on paper. Budde, Dawson, and Robinson had been first-round NFL draft picks, and Arbanas, Bell, Garrett, and Holub had all been second-rounders. NFL teams believed they could play coming out of college. Kansas City also had the most dynamic offensive weapon in this game in Taylor.

Psychologically, the Chiefs knew this aging Green Bay team was at the back end of the Lombardi dynasty, not the front end.

"We looked at their team and looked at our team," Arbanas said. "We looked at me and the Green Bay tight end, our tackles and their tackles, and right on down the line. We felt we were going to give them a helluva game. I don't think we ever went into a game thinking we were going to lose—and we didn't go into that game thinking we were going to lose."

But the Packers had been on this stage countless times before under Lombardi. This was a relatively new experience for the young Chiefs. They realized there was no room for error.

"It was one of those deals where we said if we don't make a mistake, if we don't do this, if we don't do that . . . ," Dawson said. "It was all based on playing a perfect game. If that's the case—no penalties, no interceptions, no turnovers, and we don't let them score—then, yeah, we're going to beat them. But nobody plays a perfect game."

The first error came before the game was played.

The Hammer 21

Fred Williamson was destined for Hollywood.

But first there was a nearly decade-long stay in professional football.

Williamson played his college ball at Northwestern in the late 1950s, then signed with the San Francisco 49ers in 1960 as an undrafted free agent. He was traded that summer to the Pittsburgh Steelers, with whom he spent one quiet year in the NFL, starting six games at safety with no interceptions. He changed both leagues and positions in 1961, signing with the AFL Oakland Raiders and moving to cornerback.

Williamson excelled in both places, intercepting five passes in his first season, eight in his second season, and six more in his third. He was voted to the AFL All-Star Game all three of those seasons and earned first-team All-Pro acclaim in both 1962 and 1963. He picked up the nickname "The Hammer" along the way for the physicality of his game—in particular, his neck-tie tackles when he would "drop the hammer" on receivers.

Williamson intercepted six more passes in 1964 before Raiders head coach Al Davis decided to trade him.

"I told Al, 'Trade me anywhere . . . but don't trade me to Kansas City.' It was not a night-life town," Williamson said. "It had nothing to do with [the Chiefs]. It was a dead town. I learned that from all the years I came into Kansas City to play the Chiefs."

But Kansas City would be his destination in a corner-for-corner swap with the Chiefs for Dave Grayson. Coach Hank Stram was building a defense that favored size, and Williamson provided the Chiefs a jumbo cornerback at six-three and 219 pounds. He would allow the Chiefs to physically match up better than the five-ten Grayson against two of the AFL's premier receivers in the West: six-three, 211-pound Art Powell of the

Raiders and six-two, 215-pound Lionel Taylor of the Broncos. Williamson intercepted six passes for the Chiefs in 1965 and four more in 1966.

The first AFL-NFL championship game offered Williamson the national stage he coveted. And he wasn't going to waste this opportunity in Los Angeles where he would one day earn a living.

"There were two weeks before the game, and we were staying in Long Beach," Len Dawson said. "Lombardi was smart because he didn't let the media roam freely. Today it's more organized, where the press has only an hour or so with the players. But in those days, they called your room and say, 'C'mon down to the coffee shop.' Hank Stram wanted it that way, or else it wouldn't have happened."

That was Stram's first error. Media interviews are a two-way street. Players and coaches can speak their minds on a variety of topics. But they also can hear what reporters are thinking in how they couch their questions. And the tone of the questioning at the Long Beach hotel seemed to be—*Who are you guys and what are you doing here*?

"We were the AFL, and everyone was saying, 'They're not very good... They're not very good,'" Mike Garrett said. "All the major cities were in the NFL. When you think of Chicago and Green Bay, people think, 'Oh, those are good teams.' But in the AFL we were in Denver, San Diego, Buffalo, Kansas City... People underestimated Kansas City back then. It was a town that did not strike fear in anyone."

Stram hoped to use the negative tone of the media to his benefit.

"Stram was saying, 'We've got a psychological advantage here because no one thinks we can win. The Packer players feel that way, too, so let's not do anything to get their attention," Dawson said. "Now here comes the Hammer."

Williamson talked as if Kansas City was the heavy favorite, not Green Bay. He became the go-to guy on the Chiefs for interviews—and he had plenty to say to the national media.

"I was the pied piper of that game," Williamson said. "I was the only one being verbal. I was the only talker. In athletic ethics, that's not a nice thing to do: talk about your opponent. I was saying Boyd Dowler was nothing, that he wasn't going to catch a pass on me, and if he did, I was going to try to break his neck. Carroll Dale couldn't rate with half the pass receivers in our league. At that time I was covering people like (Lance)

Alworth and (Elbert) Dubenion. I didn't think these guys had the speed or the finesse of our (AFL) guys, so I wasn't worried about them. I said they weren't going to catch anything on me, and if they did, they would pay the price. That was not a nice a thing to say."

His words raised the eyebrows of the Packers—and the Chiefs.

"The Packers weren't talking to the media much," Dawson said. "So they're over in our camp, and here's the Hammer, inviting them all over. The rest of the players were saying, 'God damn, Hammer, shut him up.' If we had a psychological advantage, it was gone."

But Williamson wasn't buying the psychological aspect of football. He didn't care what the Packers thought. Those daily sessions with the media were entertainment—a world Williamson would enter in 1968 as an actor. He would appear in more than a hundred roles in television and the movies, including guest spots on such shows as *Star Trek*, *M*A*S*H*, *Lou Grant*, and *Starsky & Hutch*.

"I was not surprised at the feedback from the sports writers because they write anything," Williamson said. "I was not surprised by the feedback from the Packers because they did not take me seriously. They said, 'Yeah, he's a good football player. We'll see how good he is on Sunday.'

"But I was surprised about the feedback I got from some of the people on my own team. They thought I was waking them up. I said, they know we're here. We know that they're there. They know that come Sunday we're going to meet each other at one o'clock on the field to find out who was the fastest draw. I wasn't waking anybody up. I was just breaking a rule—a rule of athletic ethics, which is don't talk about your opponent. But if I don't like you, why should I show respect? If I think I'm better than you, I'm not going to show you any respect. You'd have to literally beat me up consistently to get any respect from me. They hadn't done that, and I didn't think they had anybody on their team that could do that."

Frankly, Williamson was disappointed in the reaction of his teammates. He believed the Chiefs earned the right to play in this game and represent the AFL and that they should have embraced his confidence and swagger.

"They forgot what got us to the Super Bowl—the brashness of the players," Williamson said. "The Kansas City Chiefs always had good football players, All-Pros. Even when I was playing against them in Oakland. They always had great players, but they weren't champions. They weren't champions because they didn't have a leader. All they needed was a leader. When I got traded to Kansas City, I became the leader. They identified me as such by naming me captain.

"The year we went to the Super Bowl, I was the captain. I was their holler guy. I was their fire guy. I was the guy who got up and said before every game, 'These guys ain't shit. You guys are better. You guys are the All-Pros.' I said that every game. They started believing it and picking up my attitude. They took on my personality. They forgot that that's what got us there—that brashness. Respect your own ability."

But Williamson seemed alone in that belief.

"Hank pulled me off to the side and said, 'You've got to stop doing that. You've got to quiet down a little bit,'" Williamson recalled. "I told him that this is what got us here—these guys believing in themselves that they were better than the guys they were playing against. Maybe they weren't as arrogant as I was, but at least they were talking."

But, as was written in the previous chapter, Kansas City and the Chiefs were a town and team that gave African American players a home and a voice. And Williamson was going to use his.

"Hammer was ahead of his time," Dawson said. "He was Black, and the authority figure was very big in those days. Lombardi, for example. Here's Freddie, blowing his own tune and dancing to his own drummer."

And Williamson would dance right up until game time.

The Interview 22

The Kansas City Chiefs found a surprise waiting for them in their locker room when they arrived at the Los Angeles Coliseum for the inaugural AFL-NFL championship game.

Mickey Mouse ears.

The AFL had been dubbed the "Mickey Mouse League" by cynical NFL writers over the years, and at each locker was a pair of mouse ears purchased down the road at Disneyland. They came courtesy of Kansas City coach Hank Stram.

"That was just Hank trying to break the tension," Len Dawson said. "I didn't put the ears on, but I know Sherrill Headrick had one on. I think Freddie (Arbanas) did too."

"It was more of an afterthought," added Johnny Robinson. "I think Stram was trying to inspire us."

The AFL story itself was inspiring. In just seven years the AFL, with its collection of small-market teams, had brought the big-market NFL to its knees and forced a merger. The first perk in the new union was a championship game between the two leagues to conclude the 1966 season.

It was fitting that the first AFL team to play an NFL team was that of Lamar Hunt. He founded the AFL because the NFL would not allow him into enter their fraternity. The merger forced the NFL to take him and his eight AFL brethren into their fold. There's always tension in the locker room before a game, and there was certainly tension in the Kansas City locker room on this day. But it had less to do with winning than just the magnitude of the moment.

"When we got there we realized this was a historical event," Robinson said. "We experienced all the pressures of being one of the first two teams in the game. I think we were tight. Green Bay may not have felt it like we did. They were probably thinking, 'What happens if these guys beat us? What would happen then?'"

That's exactly what the Packers were thinking.

"We were clearly concerned about what we were being asked to do," Green Bay's Willie Davis said. "But at the same time we also were saying, 'After all, who else could they ask to go and do this . . . prove the point of NFL superiority?'"

Championship games were old hat for the Lombardi Packers. So were championship victories. But this one was different. The stage was much bigger, the lights much brighter, and, for the first time, the game was being played on a neutral field. There also would be two networks broadcasting the game—another first. CBS, the NFL network, featured Ray Scott, Jack Whitaker, Frank Gifford, and Pat Summerall at the microphones. NBC, the AFL network, countered with Curt Gowdy, Paul Christman, and Charlie Jones.

Gifford conducted a pre-game interview with Lombardi, his old offensive coach with the Giants, and that got the attention of the Packers.

"Giff put his arm on coach Lombardi's shoulder, and coach was shaking like a leaf," guard Jerry Kramer recalled. "I wasn't nervous until I saw how coach Lombardi was. Then that made me nervous. This [game] was not just for the Green Bay Packers or the NFL. It was for the owners of the NFL, the longterm guys who had been there forever, the heroes of coach Lombardi to a certain extent. We knew that the Halases and Maras and all the old-guard owners were putting pressure on coach Lombardi not only to win but to win big. I believe he had about as much pressure on him for that game as any he ever coached."

The pressure on the Packers wasn't coming just from the NFL owners.

"Johnny Unitas, Frank Gifford, Sam Huff, and I had all gone to Vietnam the year before on one of the NFL tours," Davis said. "I remember I got a call from Unitas teasing me about some of the things on the trip. Then he talked very quickly and very specifically about, 'Look, we're depending on you guys. Don't embarrass us. We know you guys can do it. You've got to do it.' It wasn't fun and games. It was serious. There was that potential embarrassment for every player that ever played in the NFL.

"I must have gotten a half dozen calls. Every teammate that I subsequently talked to pretty much got calls. There was no question that the rest of the league rallied around us with the sense that you've got to get it done for all of us."

The last team tasked with upholding the honor of the NFL against an upstart was the Los Angeles Rams in 1950. The All-America Football Conference (AAFC) was formed in 1946 to challenge the NFL. Like the AFL, the inaugural AAFC season fielded eight teams: the Brooklyn Dodgers, Buffalo Bills, Chicago Rockets, Cleveland Browns, Los Angeles Dons, Miami Seahawks, New York Yankees, and San Francisco 49ers.

The Seahawks dropped out after one season and were replaced by the Baltimore Colts. In 1949, the league's fourth and final season, the Brooklyn and New York franchises merged. But the AAFC essentially evolved into a one-team league—the Cleveland Browns, who posted an overall 47-4-3 record and won all four championships.

In 1950 there wasn't so much as a merger with the NFL as there was an absorption. The AAFC disbanded, and the NFL agreed to take on three of the franchises: the Browns, 49ers, and Colts. Cleveland had a great coach (Paul Brown) and a great quarterback (Otto Graham), but the NFL didn't have a feel for the talent level of the Browns. They hadn't spent the last four years playing the Bears, Eagles, and Rams. They were beating up on Dons, Rockets, and Yankees. Reality for the Browns figured to arrive in 1950.

But the Browns thumped the defending NFL champion Eagles in Philadelphia in their season opener, 35–10, and then blew through the rest of the league, tying the New York Giants for the Eastern Conference title with a 10–2 record. The Browns then defeated the Giants in a playoff, by a score of 8–3, to earn the right to play the Rams for the NFL championship.

Los Angeles captured the Western Conference with a 9–3 record to advance to the NFL championship game for the second consecutive season. The Rams fielded an offense that featured two Hall of Fame quarterbacks, Norm Van Brocklin and Bob Waterfield, and two Hall of Fame receivers, Tom Fears and Elroy "Crazy Legs" Hirsch, to defend the honor of the NFL. But Graham rallied the Browns from an 8-point fourth-quarter deficit to topple the Rams, 30–28, winning on a Lou Groza field goal in the final minute.

So much for NFL superiority. Could the Chiefs follow in the footsteps of the Browns sixteen years later?

"Vince was very nervous before the game," Davis said. "What he said clearly came out of his own sense of where he was and where we were. He went through his usual pre-game [spiel] of what we can't do—'We can't let them do this, can't let them do that, can't let Dawson get hot, can't let Dawson get out of the pocket . . .' He called Mike Garrett that darting runner and said, 'We've got to shut off those things. We can't let them get encouraged early.' Kansas City was a pretty awesome-looking football team. They got our attention."

But beyond the pressure on Lombardi coming from the ownership of other NFL teams, the Packers needed to win this game for themselves. Their own legacy was at stake—not to mention that fat game check.

"There was a combination of pride in our team and in ourselves," Kramer said, "and the $15,000 was a big thing at that time. The losers got maybe $7,500. That was almost double my salary, so it was a big payoff day. That was important.

"But the pride of the Green Bay Packers—the history of who we were and what we were and what we were doing against a team we didn't know—was a factor. We wanted the world to see the Green Bay Packers. We were proud of our performance, our record, our team—everything about us. This game was a culmination of many things."

There wasn't a team familiarity in this game but there certainly were individual familiarities. Kansas City offensive lineman Jon Gilliam was drafted by Green Bay in 1960 and spent training camp that summer with the Packers. Fred Williamson played a game against Starr, Taylor, and the Packers in his one NFL season in 1960. Nine Chiefs—Reg Carolan, Wayne Frazier, Curtis McClinton, Bobby Ply, Bobby Bell, Buck Buchanan, Ed Budde, Aaron Brown, and Mike Garrett—played against the Packers in the various College All-Star Games. Fred Arbanas had been a college teammate of Herb Adderley at Michigan State. Adderley, in fact, gave Arbanas two of his tickets for the championship game that day.

Johnny Robinson had been a college teammate of Jim Taylor at LSU. The two were best friends.

Not that it mattered to Taylor.

"It was just another game, like an NFL game," said Taylor, of what would be his final appearance as a Packer. "I played in four or five of those (championship) games. You can hype it and say what you want about it, but it's the same people no matter what color the jersey. The ball's the same. The players with the guts to play under pressure are the winners. The guys who are in the open but don't tense up and catch the ball are the winners. The ones who drop it are the losers. You keep putting the pressure on until they either break or they break you. That's what competition is. We defied people to stop us."

But the better question might have been, could the Packers stop the highest-scoring team in football? The honor of the NFL was at stake.

Fig. 23. A young Lamar Hunt

Fig. 24. Lamar Hunt

Fig. 25. Cornerback Emmitt Thomas

Fig. 26. Fullback Mack Lee Hill runs off tackle against the Oakland Raiders

Fig. 27. Defensive back and HBCU product Fletcher Smith

Fig. 28. Mike Garrett (21) and Otis Taylor (89) celebrate a Kansas City touchdown

Fig. 29. Kansas City Chiefs in front row: Johnny Robinson (42), Hank Stram, Len Dawson (16). Second row: Bobby Bell (78), Ed Budde (71), Jim Tyrer (77), Buck Buchanan (86), Jerry Mays (75), Fred Arbanas (84), Otis Taylor (89)

Fig. 30. Quarterback Len Dawson throws a pass in the Super Bowl against the Packers

Fig. 31. Dallas Texans in front row: Max Boydston (81), Jerry Cornelison (74), Billy Krisher (64), Jon Gilliam (65), Al Reynolds (60), Jim Tyrer (77), Chris Burford (88). Second row: Lamar Hunt, Johnny Robinson (42), Bo Dickinson (32), Cotton Davidson (19), Abner Haynes (28), Hank Stram

Fig. 32. Tight end Fred Arbanas (84) visits with Green Bay cornerback Herb Adderley after the Super Bowl

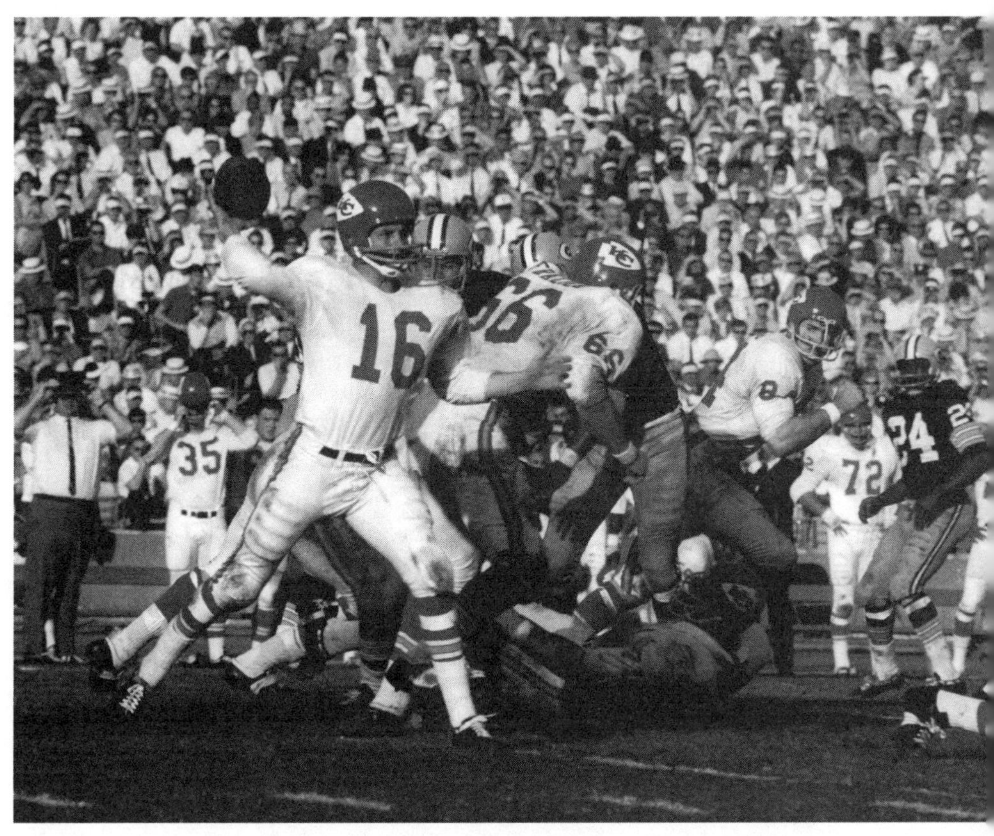

Fig. 33. Quarterback Len Dawson (16) throws a pass against the Packers in the Super Bowl

Fig. 34. Lamar Hunt, Hank Stram, and club president Jack Steadman

Fig. 35. Dallas Texans quarterback Cotton Davidson (19) throwing a pass on the run

Fig. 36. Coach Hank Stram surrounded by Auburn alums Dave Hill (73), Bobby Hunt (20), Chuck Hurston (85), and Wayne Frazier (66)

Fig. 37. Fullback Mack Lee Hill

Fig. 38. Cornerback Fred Williamson

Fig. 39. Offense in pregame warmups at Municipal Stadium

Fig. 40. E. J. Holub in a postgame interview after a victory over the San Diego Chargers

Fig. 41. Sitting on the bench in the first season in Kansas City in 1963: Chris Burford (88), Abner Haynes (28), Charley Diamond (79), Jim Tyrer (77), Fred Arbanas (84), and Johnny Robinson (42)

Fig. 42. Lamar Hunt

Fig. 43. Len Dawson under pressure in the pocket in the Super Bowl versus the Packers

Fig. 44. Kansas City Chiefs cheerleader

23 Hope

The Los Angeles Coliseum was not a new venue for the Kansas City Chiefs.

The franchise played its very first AFL game there in 1960, then as the Dallas Texans, falling to the Los Angeles Chargers, 21–20, before a crowd of 17,724. The crowd would be considerably larger for the franchise's next visit to the Coliseum in 1967.

As an NFL facility—the Los Angeles Rams had called the Coliseum home since 1946—the Packers were the designated home team for the first Super Bowl. But the Kansas City Chiefs did not feel like visitors when they trotted onto the field for the pre-game warmups. Something very familiar was waiting for them: painted end zones.

After the merger of the two leagues was announced in 1966, NFL commissioner Pete Rozelle traveled to Kansas City in November to attend his first AFL game. He saw gold end zones at Municipal Stadium with the word "Chiefs" painted red in them. His own league had fourteen sets of grassy green end zones. The color in the Kansas City end zones added some flair to the setting.

So Rozelle commissioned Kansas City groundskeeper George Toma to paint the end zones for the first Super Bowl. And, as it has turned out, every Super Bowl thereafter. One gold end zone was adorned with "Chiefs" in red and the AFL logo, the other gold end zone with "Packers" in green and the NFL logo.

The Packers had some familiarity with the building as well. Green Bay had closed the regular season in the Coliseum less than a month earlier, defeating the Rams 27–23. So the Super Bowl was the second time in a span of three games the Packers would play in Los Angeles.

But the game seemed more of a curiosity than an event to the Hollywood crowd.

On November 26, 1966, 88,520 fans turned out at the Coliseum to see Notre Dame clinch a national championship with a 51–0 thumping of Southern Cal. Seven weekends later, only 61,949 filled the same building to see the first Super Bowl. That's 26,571 empty seats—at an average of just twelve dollars per ticket.

Still, it was the largest crowd ever to see the Chiefs play. Only one other time in its seven-year history had the franchise played before a crowd of sixty thousand—when the Chiefs visited the New York Jets the previous November.

But big crowds were routine for the Packers. Green Bay played in front of eighty-three thousand in a September game in Cleveland, seventy-two thousand at the College All-Star Game in Chicago in August, and seventy-four thousand in the NFL championship game in Dallas. The Packers won all three of the games, all as the visitors.

Emmitt Thomas was a rookie cornerback with the Chiefs in 1966 but played sparingly behind Willie Mitchell and Fred Williamson. His role was on special teams, returning and covering kicks. As the Chiefs filed into the Coliseum tunnel for the pre-game introductions, Thomas saw something that surprised him.

"Everyone was crying—Buck Buchanan, Jerry Mays, E. J. Holub, Chris Burford, Bobby Bell, Otis . . . ," Thomas said. "I asked, 'What are you crying about? We haven't even started the game yet.' I was a rookie and didn't understand the significance of the game. I was just so happy to be there. But they understood the significance. This was their chance to prove our league was legitimate, our players were legitimate."

It was a perfect day for football—sunny and 72°F. The Chiefs wore white jerseys over white pants, and the Packers wore their green jerseys over gold pants. The bespeckled Vince Lombardi wore a white short-sleeved shirt and a tie—easily recognizable to a national television audience that had watched him and his Packers win four previous NFL championship games. Stram wore a black blazer with a red Chiefs logo on the pocket as if to identify himself as the Kansas City coach to a far-less familiar television audience.

The Packers won the coin toss and elected to receive. So the first player ever to touch a football in a Super Bowl was an HBCU product—Tennessee State's Fletcher Smith, who kicked off for Kansas City. He also was the team's fourth cornerback.

The Packers opened the way you'd expect a Lombardi team to start: running the ball on the first three downs, including halfback Elijah Pitts carrying on the famed "Packer power sweep" with pulling guards Jerry Kramer and Fuzzy Thurston in front of him. On the third play of the game, Green Bay split end Boyd Dowler threw a crackback block on Kansas City safety Johnny Robinson at the line of scrimmage but injured his shoulder as he fell to the ground. He trotted off the field favoring his right side and was done for the day.

"We really got a lucky break when their best receiver went out on the third play of the game," Johnny Robinson said. "So we were playing against a backup."

Green Bay quarterback Bart Starr targeted that backup, Max McGee, with his first pass of the game on the very next play, but underthrew him on a crossing route. That left the Packers in an obvious passing situation on second-and-10.

Fuzzy Thurston was in his eighth season as the starting left guard on the Packers. At six-one, 247 pounds, he was giving away six inches and forty pounds to the player lined up across from him. And Buck Buchanan blew through Thurston on the way to Starr for a 10-yard sack.

On the next play, Buchanan slid over and lined up over center Bill Curry. It was another physical mismatch—Curry stood six-three and weighed 235. But a blitzing Bobby Bell used a speed rush from the right side to get to Starr first for a second consecutive sack and a loss of 5 more yards.

Fourth-and-25 six plays into the game was not how Lombardi expected to start off in his bid to school the AFL champions.

On Kansas City's first possession, the Chiefs employed their moving pocket with Dawson drifting left away from the Davis-Robinson-Adderley defensive triangle on the right side. Chris Burford caught Dawson's pass on the left sideline, but it was ruled incomplete because he stepped out of bounds.

Dave Robinson saw something on that play that troubled him. With

Kansas City's moving pocket, Dawson was slowing the pass rush and sending his two running backs out as receivers. The Packers weren't expecting it.

"After the very first play," Robinson said, "we told our defensive coordinator (Phil Bengtson), 'They're running five-man patterns. We can't stay in the defense we're in.'

"In our defense, I provided underneath coverage to Herb Adderley. I shadowed them. They would have to throw over me. After 10 yards, Herb would pick them up. Our linebacking corps was one of the best in football at underneath coverage. But when they ran five-man patterns, I had a man. I couldn't shadow for Herb. Our whole defense broke down because our defensive backs had no underneath coverage from the linebackers. We told Phil, and he said, 'They can't be.' We said they are. And Phil said, we'll check on it at halftime."

Dawson threw his first three passes at Burford, targeting Green Bay cornerback Bob Jeter, before finally launching a pass over the head of Otis Taylor on a third-and-14. This time the Chiefs were forced to punt.

It was like the first round of a prize fight—a lot of sparring but few haymakers.

"Sometimes you'd be doing the trash talking because you knew you had an edge," Willie Davis said. "In a typical game, I'd probably say something just to try to get a reaction. I might say, 'Hey, (Kansas City offensive tackle Dave) Hill. This is going to be a pass.' A lot of times guys would make an unconscious adjustment if they think you caught them in something. Many times I was unsure myself. But if I said something, it would make him make some adjustment that would tell me yea or nay. That would determine how I would come off the ball. It was all a bit of a mind game.

"But I don't think I said one word to Hill the entire first half."

With 9:10 remaining in the opening quarter, the Packers finally showed up. The Lombardi Packers. The Green Bay team that had dominated the NFL for the last six years, winning 79.1 percent of its games and those four championships.

It took the Packers just six plays to cover 80 yards for a 7–0 lead. Starr completed all four of his passes for 82 yards. His last pass was behind McGee on a crossing route, but he reached back and stabbed it with his left hand at the Kansas City 23 and jogged untouched into the end zone to complete the 37-yard play.

With 5:54 remaining in the quarter, the Chiefs finally showed up. The Stram Chiefs. The Kansas City offense that disarmed AFL defenses with its creativity. Distributing the ball to five different teammates, Dawson marched Kansas City 72 yards in nine plays to the Green Bay 15 only to see Mike Mercer's 40-yard field goal attempt sail wide left.

But Stram's moving pocket came into play in slowing the Green Bay pass rush. Dawson dropped back seven times and drifted left away from Willie Davis five times. But the one Chief who wasn't involved in the offense was Taylor, who was being occupied by Adderley and safety Tom Brown. Dawson threw five passes at Burford in the first two possessions but only one at Taylor. The Packers were fine with that ball distribution.

"Chris couldn't beat you deep," said Emmitt Thomas, who had covered Burford and Taylor daily in practice that season. "All he could do was catch the outs, the quick slants, and the curls. He had a nice double move to go deep, but he was more a possession-type receiver."

The Packers knew they weren't going to get beaten with possession routes. The more passes Dawson threw to Burford, the more comfortable the Packers became on defense. Their focus was keeping Taylor out of the end zone. So every pass to Burford, Arbanas, and Garrett was a victory for the Green Bay defense.

But the highest-scoring team in the AFL was just warming up on offense. For the remainder of the half, the Chiefs sliced through the Packers as if they were the Dolphins or Patriots. A three-and-out by the Packers set the Chiefs up at their own 34. Six plays later, Kansas City was in the end zone, and the game was tied at 7–7.

Dawson took his moving pocket right on the first play and hit Garrett for a 17-yard gain. But it was all Garrett who caught the pass in the left flat and then raced across the field. Ray Nitschke, Lee Roy Caffey, Davis, and Robinson all got arms or hands on him but couldn't bring him down. After three runs, Dawson again went play-action, finally finding Taylor on a post-flag route for 31 yards to the Green Bay 7.

On the next snap, another play-action, Dawson faked a handoff to Garrett running left with fullback Curtis McClinton as his lead blocker.

Garrett was tackled, but McClinton kept right on going into the front corner of the end zone where he was open for a 7-yard Dawson touchdown pass. The Chiefs covered those 66 yards in six plays.

Kansas City got the ball back with four minutes left in the half and this time marched 74 yards in eight plays to the Green Bay 24, setting up a 31-yard field goal by Mercer. Dawson completed all four of his passes in the drive to four different receivers—a 12-yarder to Arbanas, an 11-yarder to Taylor, a 27-yarder to Burford, and an 8-yarder to Garrett.

But in between those two Kansas City scores, the Packers put together a 73-yard touchdown drive of their own in thirteen plays, mixing run with pass. Green Bay actually scored twice in the possession. On a third-and-1 at the Green Bay 36, with the Chiefs bunched at the line anticipating a plunge from Taylor, Starr dropped back and threw a dart to a wide-open Carroll Dale, who raced down the middle of the field 64 yards, untouched, for a touchdown. But premature movement along the Green Bay offensive line drew a penalty flag for illegal procedure, wiping out the score.

Eleven plays later, though, Taylor swept left end on another power sweep. Pulling guards Kramer and Thurston took out Sherrill Headrick and Johnny Robinson with blocks, and Taylor scooted 14 yards into the end zone.

So the Packers led at halftime, 14–10. That wasn't a surprise. The surprise was the dominance in the half by the AFL champion. Kansas City averaged 6.46 yards per play in the half and managed more first downs, more yards, more passing yards, more sacks on defense, and fewer punts than Green Bay. The last three times Kansas City touched the ball in the half, they drove 72, 66, and 73 yards through one of the NFL's best defenses.

Dawson wasn't playing like an NFL washout, completing 11-of-15 passes for 152 yards with a touchdown. Stram's moving pocket and a heavy dose of play-action was slowing the Green Bay pass rush. The Chiefs utilized the floating pocket eleven times and the play-action eight times in the half. The Packers didn't know if Dawson had the ball nor did they know where to find him.

Garrett caught a team-high three passes in the half and was giving the Packers fits with his speed and shiftiness underneath. Buchanan was terrorizing the interior of the Green Bay offensive line. He sacked Starr once and drilled the Green Bay quarterback in the chest on a rollout another time. And now the Packers were two starters down on offense. Dowler left in the first quarter, and Ken Bowman replaced Bill Curry at center in the second quarter.

The momentum was with the Chiefs—and they would receive the second half kickoff with the chance to take the lead.

Adjustments 24

While the college marching bands of the University of Arizona and Grambling State were entertaining the Super Bowl crowd on the field at halftime, Vince Lombardi was bellowing in the Green Bay locker room beneath the Coliseum.

"Vince was yelling, 'What's wrong with you guys? What's wrong with you guys? And blah, blah, blah . . .'" recalled Green Bay's Dave Robinson.

This wasn't how the Super Bowl was supposed to play out. The Packers were expected to assert their superiority and that of their league by steamrolling the AFL champion Chiefs from start to finish. The Packers were 14-point favorites, and a thrashing along the lines of Green Bay's 31–7 thumping of the Detroit Lions in October was expected.

But the Chiefs were surprisingly competitive and trailed the Packers by a mere 4 points at halftime.

"I wasn't surprised the score was close at half," Herb Adderley said. "We knew we were going to win, but we knew we had to make some adjustments. We were feeling them out in the first half."

There was no yelling over in the Kansas City locker room. The Chiefs were almost giddy and brimming with confidence at their performance over the first thirty minutes.

"I remember the elation of the players in the locker room, the emotion," Len Dawson said. "To that point all the talk about beating the Packers was lip service. But at halftime, we really believed it. We felt we were going to pull off the biggest upset in the history of sports. We were the underdogs—and we were the only ones who remotely felt we had a chance. Now we believed it ourselves. We really felt we could pull it off."

The Chiefs knew they were younger and faster than the Packers. They also knew they had some size advantages. But there were a few issues.

Foremost among them was cornerback Willie Mitchell, who was burned twice by aging backup receiver Max McGee, who caught only four passes during the regular season. The Packers gained only 164 yards in the first half, and McGee had 47 of them on two receptions.

Mitchell's teammates were supportive both on the sideline and in the locker room at halftime, and he assured them, "I'll get it going . . . I'll get it going."

And they were sure Mitchell would. He spent the last few seasons covering the AFL's best in Lance Alworth, Don Maynard, George Sauer, Elbert Dubenion, Lionel Taylor, and Art Powell. McGee may have been in their class in 1961 when he went to his only Pro Bowl, but at thirty-five years of age in this Super Bowl, he was in the waning moments of his career.

Still, the Chiefs discovered the Packers were not only beatable—they were human.

"They weren't fancy," Johnny Robinson said. "They were plain. Nothing Green Bay did surprised us. We knew exactly what they were going to run. They were a power-type team, but their backs were slow. They weren't as fast as our linebackers."

The Chiefs couldn't wait to get back onto the field. Neither could the Packers.

"The first half was kind of ho-hum," Jerry Kramer said. "We got a little acquainted with E. J. Holub, Bobby Bell, Johnny Robinson, Buck Buchanan . . . They had some really good football players."

"They were clearly better than they were initially given credit for," added Willie Davis. "Had they gone into halftime in the lead, I think they would have been a very different football team. They really were in a position that that could have happened."

But it didn't happen. The Packers were on the top side of the scoreboard and, with a few adjustments, expected to remain there.

"We couldn't get into our defense the whole half," Dave Robinson said.

The first adjustment would come on Kansas City's passing downs. After the offense and defense broke off in groups at halftime, Green Bay defensive coordinator Phil Bengtson surveyed his coverage troops.

"Phil asked, 'What's your man doing . . . What's your man doing . . . What's your man doing?'" Robinson recalled. "Finally he says, 'Wait a minute—they're running five-man patterns.' And we said, 'That's what we've been telling you. What are we going to do?' And Phil said, 'What do they do when we blitz?' And Willie Wood said, 'Coach, we didn't blitz the whole first half, not one time.' So Phil said, 'We'll correct that. When they show pass, we're going to blitz them.'"

The second adjustment was to address Kansas City's moving pocket. The pass rush was not getting to Dawson because the Green Bay front four didn't know where to find him. He could sprint out to the right and set up to pass. Or he could go left. Or he could throw off a three-step drop. He even took the occasional seven-step drop. There was no predictability on passing downs.

"I had definitely played much more conservative because of the floating pocket," Davis said. "I was not as eager to gamble."

So Adderley offered up a suggestion.

"When they started rolling to my side, which was the left side along with Willie and Dave, they were cracking back on Davis, and he couldn't get out to force Dawson to throw the ball," Adderley said. "Dave was back in pass coverage, so they had more time than we really wanted to give them.

"I suggested that Dave get into Willie's spot in a two-point stance at the defensive-end position, and that set Davis out further, split from Robinson in a three-point stance. All he had to do was rush the passer from there. We talked about it at halftime and decided to try it. That forced Dawson to stay in the pocket and throw the ball quicker. Robinson—with his size, height, and speed—could still play the end run or the slant, yet when he recognized a pass, he could get back in the flat and the hook zone. Davis had nothing to do but rush the passer. He didn't have to worry about any pass coverage, he just had to make sure Dawson didn't get outside the pocket."

The Packers were minimizing Otis Taylor in the Kansas City offense and were employing a successful strategy against the tight end Fred Arbanas as well. He was voted first-team All-Pro in 1966 and caught a touchdown pass against the Buffalo Bills in the AFL title game.

"Arbanas had been Herb's tight end at Michigan State," Dave Robinson said. "He'd tell me how big and strong he was, how he could do this and do that. Herb thought he was the greatest thing since bubble gum. So I jammed him off the ball. And we knew about his (left) eye. When we watched film, if he caught ten balls eight of them were to the one side. So Vince told us to overplay the side of his good eye, and we shut him down."

With the halftime adjustments in place, Lombardi again addressed his team before the Packers were summoned back to the field. When their head coach spoke, the Packers listened.

"Lombardi made one statement that, in my opinion, completely turned the game," Davis said. "He said, 'Okay, you've gone out and played thirty minutes of football adjusting to the Kansas City Chiefs. All I'm asking you to do now is play thirty minutes of football the way you can play it, and let's see if they can adjust to us.' The attitude just changed with him making that statement."

And just as the Kansas City offense took charge of the game in the second quarter, the Green Bay defense would take charge in the third quarter.

25 The Interception

NBC was granted a mulligan at the start of the second half of the first Super Bowl. Len Dawson was not.

The Kansas City Chiefs were anxious to get started because they brought carryover momentum from the second quarter and were scheduled to receive the football to start the second half with a chance to take the lead. Don Chandler kicked off for Green Bay, but before the Chiefs could return the ball, the play was whistled dead.

Both CBS and NBC were broadcasting the game and shared a singular video feed from CBS. But when Chandler kicked off, NBC was still in a commercial break, which necessitated the restart of the half and the re-kick.

Bert Coan returned the second kickoff 16 yards to the Kansas City 29. On first down, Dawson created a floating pocket to his right but under pressure escaped the containment of Dave Robinson and scrambled for 15 yards around end. The Chiefs then ran the ball twice up the middle, first with fullback Curtis McClinton and then halfback Mike Garrett. They gained 5 yards, placing the Chiefs in a third-and-5 at midfield—an obvious passing situation.

"Phil (defensive coordinator Bengtson) signaled a three-man blitz—all three linebackers," Green Bay's Dave Robinson said. "We got into the huddle, and Nitschke's smiling, Caffey is jabbering, and I'm happy."

The Chiefs saw no need to change their offensive strategy in the second half. The play-action, moving pocket, five-receiver calls were working. The Green Bay defense was, well, on the defensive. So it would be more of the same in the third quarter from the Chiefs.

At the snap, running backs McClinton and Garrett flared out to the right in the five-receiver pattern with hopes of drawing the Green Bay linebackers in coverage to that side of the field. Dawson's intention was to throw left to tight end Fred Arbanas on a short sideline square-out pattern. Dawson hoped his eyes, looking right at Otis Taylor and his running backs, would draw the safeties leaning in that direction.

But on this play, the Packers were not going to let Dawson dictate what they should do. It was Green Bay's turn to start dictating. Lee Roy Caffey raced in from the left side of the formation, Robinson came charging from the right, and end Lionel Aldridge and tackle Henry Jordan collapsed the pass protection from the inside. Four Packers were on top of Dawson before he could even finish his drop.

"His eyes were as big as saucers," Robinson said, "and he threw up a wounded duck."

The pass fluttered in the direction of Arbanas—but it was slightly underthrown and behind him. Safety Willie Wood intercepted the pass in stride and kept right on running to the 5-yard line where Garrett finally dragged him down.

With five receivers in the pattern, there was no one left in the backfield to protect Dawson from the onslaught. The Chiefs were asking five linemen up front to block the seven Packers in the pass rush on that play. Caffey would normally engage Arbanas at the line of scrimmage but disregarded the Kansas City tight end to blitz.

"It was one of those plays when immediately after the ball left my hand, I knew only bad things could happen," Dawson said. "Ordinarily, you wouldn't leave yourself unprotected to that side. But the Packers never blitzed. Very seldom. They guessed right on that particular play. And the ball was floating out there."

One play later, the Chiefs were doomed. Elijah Pitts powered in off left tackle for a touchdown and a 21–10 Green Bay lead. Instead of taking the lead as the Chiefs were hoping at the start of the half, Kansas City now found itself two scores down.

"The interception was tough for me to swallow," Dawson said. "We were on the move. We took the second-half kickoff and were at midfield. We knew if we got behind and had to throw the football, it was going to be one heck of a problem for us. And that's exactly what happened. The interception, they score . . . Now we're down by 11, and we've got to play catch-up."

That eliminated the play-action pass from the Kansas City playbook. The Chiefs had the best rushing attack in pro football that season, but it no longer mattered. The Packers didn't have to honor the run any more—not when their opponent needed to score two touchdowns to get back into the game. Dawson had to pass, and the Packers knew it.

So Green Bay became more aggressive in its pass rush. That minimized the effectiveness of the moving pocket. The eyes of the Packers—and their pass rush—would now dog Dawson's every step. The strategic advantages the Chiefs enjoyed in the first half were now gone.

Another productive kickoff return by Coan gave Kansas City possession at its own 30. The Chiefs only threw three passes at Otis Taylor, their primary offensive weapon, in the first half. But Dawson threw back-to-back passes to Taylor to start their second possession of the second half. His first pass was low, and Taylor caught the second one for 11 yards. But Adderley took him down with a violent clothesline tackle.

The next time Kansas City got the ball, Dawson overthrew Chris Burford deep and then was sacked on consecutive plays—the first by Caffey and Davis and then by Henry Jordan and Ron Kostelnik. Dawson's problems continued on Kansas City's opening possession of the fourth quarter. He threw back-to-back passes, but the first was almost intercepted by Wood, and the second was almost intercepted by Adderley.

In the meantime, Green Bay built its lead to 28–10 on its final possession of the third quarter. McGee caught three passes in the 56-yard, ten-play drive, including a 13-yard touchdown pass. Like his first touchdown, this was also a circus catch. McGee stabbed the high throw with his left hand for a juggling catch in the end zone.

McGee caught seven passes for 138 yards in the game—both his first 100-yard game and first two-touchdown game since 1964.

"I went into the Louisiana state Hall of Fame with Max," Johnny Robinson said. "The guy that introduced us was talking about his playboy style and said Max didn't anticipate playing (in the Super Bowl) and didn't come in until four o'clock in the morning. But he came in and had his greatest day. He wasn't their best receiver . . . but he was the best receiver on the field that day."

The Chiefs knew going into the game that there was a softness on the left side of their defense, and it had nothing to do with cornerback

Willie Mitchell. It had to do with Chuck Hurston, who led Kansas City in sacks that season with five and a half—but that was as a 240-pound weakside end.

"Chuck got sick with a virus and lost about twenty pounds right before the game," Robinson said. "He couldn't hold anything down in his stomach. In the Super Bowl, he weighed about 205 pounds—and he's playing over a guy (Green Bay offensive captain Bob Skoronski) who weighed 270 pounds and was a fine football player. We needed to give Chuck some help."

So the Chiefs blitzed Holub more on the left side to both force the run and rush the passer. That required Robinson to fill in for Holub in pass coverage, handling the running backs underneath. That took Robinson, one of the game's best ballhawks, out of the deep zone and the coverage support he would normally provide Mitchell.

"So I was out of the picture," Robinson said, "and three times they caught Willie Mitchell by himself."

Green Bay's three rushing touchdowns in the game were all to the left side, and two of them were directly behind the blocking of Skoronski.

As the Chiefs sensed the game slipping away, frustration heightened and tempers flared. On Green Bay's second touchdown drive of the third quarter, Buchanan gave Taylor a bearhug on a line plunge, but the Green Bay fullback wouldn't go down. When Taylor threw an elbow at Buchanan to free himself after the whistle, the Kansas City defensive tackle tossed him to the turf.

"I remember that play very distinctly," said Buchanan years later. "I said something, he said something, and I grabbed him. I was so angry. I still see that picture sometimes. When I see Ray Nitschke, he teases me about that. He says, 'Hey, you threw my man Jimmy down . . . just threw him down like he was nothing. You embarrassed him.' But he didn't retaliate. That was kind of surprising."

Starr threw an interception by Mitchell on Green Bay's first possession of the fourth quarter on another deep pass intended for McGee. But the Chiefs could not capitalize on the turnover. On their second possession, the Packers moved 80 yards on eight plays for the game's final score. By this time the Chiefs had flipped their cornerbacks, putting Mitchell on Carroll Dale. But Dale caught two passes in the drive for 32 yards. Elijah

Pitts made it 35–10 with his second touchdown of the game, another short plunge over left tackle.

Dawson struggled the entire second half, completing only 5-of-12 passes for 59 yards with that interception. Years later, Dave Robinson participated in Dawson's annual golf tournament in Ohio.

"Len told me that after the interception, he went to the sideline and told Hank Stram, 'They're blitzing now,'" Robinson recalled. "So Hank told him, 'Let's go back to our two- and three-man patterns.' That would give Dawson some help blocking. But they had been practicing for two weeks against our defense with five-man patterns. So when they went back to the two-man patterns, the timing was off. They hadn't run those patterns for two weeks."

With 6:13 remaining in the game and his team trailing by 25 points, Stram pulled Dawson in favor of his backup Pete Beathard.

"That was embarrassing," Dawson said. "Even more so than a pitcher being relieved."

The final indignity came in the closing minutes after the Packers had flooded the field with reserves. Donny Anderson took a handoff on a sweep of right end, and cornerback Fred Williamson charged up in run support. Gale Gillingham blocked him, and teammate Sherrill Headrick fell on him. Everyone got up after the play except Williamson, who had to be carried off the field on a stretcher.

The Hammer got hammered.

"We looked over on the other sideline, and they are laughing, telling jokes over there, talking about the Hammer," Dawson said. "It mattered so much to us . . . then to be laughed at like that. Losing to the Packers—I don't think it would have been embarrassing to anybody if it hadn't been such a lopsided affair. Particularly in the second half when they shut us out."

It marked the first time since November 6—and only the third time all season—that the Chiefs had gone consecutive quarters without scoring a point. But Kansas City had no answer for McGee on defense and no answer for those second-half blitzes on offense. A conservative Green Bay defense sacked Dawson once in the first half. An aggressive Green Bay defense sacked Dawson and Beathard five times in the second half.

"I thought the key thing about that game was our youth," Dawson said. "Nobody had ever been in a big game like that. I was the senior member of that football team, and I had never been through it. We were so young. We ran in peaks and valleys because of our youth. If something bad came, we sank down there. If something good came, we rose up there. They could handle adversity better than we could.

"Looking back at it now, it could have been to our disadvantage at halftime getting so excited. Instead of saying, 'We can do this if we just stay calm. We've got a job to do. Another thirty minutes.' It wasn't that way. It was jubilation. It was like we just discovered they were human. They can be beaten. But they had only been beaten two to three times that year."

The Packers finished their season with a seven-game winning streak. Green Bay also extended its postseason winning streak under Lombardi to six games. And that was the difference between the NFL champion and the AFL champion.

"We knew how to win," Davis said. "It wasn't a case of being the physically superior team as it was just knowing how to win. You knew how to play. We were winning as a team then. Lombardi had spent all those years preparing us how to win. We played the first half not to lose. But we played the second half absolutely to win.

"When we walked out of the Coliseum, even though it probably had not been one of our greatest games, there was no question in our mind that we had accomplished our No. 1 objective—that we had beaten the best team in the AFL by a 35–10 score."

The Sting of Defeat 26

Vince Lombardi attempted to be diplomatic immediately following Green Bay's destruction of the AFL champions in the first Super Bowl.

But he also knew what the NFL press wanted, so Lombardi gave it to them.

"I think the Kansas City team is a real tough football team," the Green Bay coach said at his postgame press conference. "But it doesn't compare with the National Football League teams. That's what you want me to say. I've said it."

But the Chiefs weren't as convinced of that as Lombardi.

"Frankly, after the game was over, I said I'd like to play them again," Mike Garrett claimed. "They weren't as good as I thought they'd be. If we didn't have that interception, we'd still have been in there fighting the rest of the way."

Another AFL team wanted a shot at the Packers as well—the Buffalo Bills. But the two-time defending AFL champion Bills blew their chance when they lost at home to the Chiefs in the league championship game. But the Bills believed they would have been a better representative in the first Super Bowl than the Chiefs.

"We matched up much better than Kansas City did from a defensive standpoint against the Packers," Buffalo cornerback Butch Byrd said. "We were much better against the run, and that's what Green Bay did with Taylor and Hornung. I'd like to think we would have won.

"We owned San Diego during those days, and I always thought that man-for-man, the Chargers had the best team in football. Lowe, Alworth, Hadl, Mix, Lincoln, Ladd, Faison . . . they had the talent. They were more wide open. But we steamrolled them. Green Bay was strong, but I think we would have shut them down. My emotions may be guiding my thoughts. But I felt confident that we'd win that game."

Kansas City quarterback Len Dawson said the Chiefs would need to play a perfect game to beat the Packers. They didn't. They committed only one turnover—the interception by Wood—and it cost them their momentum and, eventually, the game. But that's how the Packers had been feasting on NFL competition for years. You make a mistake and the Packers pounce.

"At the end of the day, it's who can execute better," Willie Davis said. "That's what Lombardi used to remind us—you can get excited, you can put in all these trick plays and do all of these things. But in the final analysis it comes down to which team executes the best."

Green Bay may have been 25 points better than Kansas City on the scoreboard. But the Chiefs didn't believe there was that much of a disparity in talent on the field.

"I've got a film of the game, and I've watched it a hundred times," said Chris Burford, who caught four passes for a team-best 67 yards. "It was there for us. I'd have loved to have played the Packers in a best two-out-of-three. I wasn't in awe of any of them. I thought we had better players at different positions than they had. But the problem was we got behind. The one thing about the Packers—it's hard to play catch up against them.

"They were a solid team, good players, but not overwhelming. I never felt I couldn't get open or I couldn't do this or do that. I don't know if some of the guys were overwhelmed because they were the Packers. I didn't get that feeling at all. They were a good team. But the Chargers were a good team. Houston was a good team. I always felt bad about that game. I wished we could have played them again the next day. But it doesn't work that way."

Green Bay carried a heavy burden into the game. Vince Lombardi and the Packers had been the face of the 1960s NFL. They were the heavy favorite in this game and expected to demonstrate the superiority of the NFL. But the Chiefs also carried a heavy burden into the game. They were hoping to prove the AFL belonged on the same field with the NFL. They failed.

"It was embarrassing," Dawson said. "It was in front of so many people.

Most athletes can handle defeat because you go through it. It happens in everyone's career. But the embarrassment . . . People said, 'You really are a Mickey Mouse league . . . no contest . . . You guys couldn't handle adversity . . . That second half the real team came to the front.' That's what was so tough to swallow."

The one player the Packers feared—Otis Taylor—was hardly a factor in the game. He caught only four passes for 57 yards. He was supposed to be the best wide receiver on the field that day, but instead it was ancient Max McGee. In hindsight, Taylor's absence was the major flaw in the Kansas City game plan.

"It probably should have geared more toward getting the ball to Otis as much as we tried to get the ball to the halfbacks and fullbacks," Dawson said.

The Chiefs were the highest-scoring team in all of football that fall with 479 points in fifteen games. The 10 points against the Packers were the fewest they scored in a game all season. But even if Kansas City had hit its average of 32 points in the game, that still wouldn't have been enough to top the 35 points the Packers registered on the scoreboard.

Stram was a brilliant offensive mind and knew the problems the Chiefs had on offense against the Packers were fixable. He knew he'd have Dawson, Garrett, McClinton, Taylor, Buford, Arbanas, and that immense offensive line all back in 1967. There would be some minor tinkering but not a major overhaul. The same could not be said for the defense.

Kansas City had some great players on that side of the ball in Buchanan, Bell, and Robinson. The Chiefs just didn't have *enough* great ones. The Packers started six defenders in the Super Bowl who would finish their careers with busts in Canton. The Chiefs started four players on defense who began their careers as undrafted free agents. It showed. The Packers converted nine of fourteen third-down situations in the Super Bowl and gained 100 yards more than the Chiefs.

"We wanted to win because that was the only time the Super Bowl was a pure game—it was pure AFL versus pure NFL," Lamar Hunt said. "By the next year we had a common draft, so there was a dissolution factor. In retrospect, we were not good enough defensively to stop the Packers. We felt we could score with them. We just couldn't stop them."

All that made for a torturous offseason for the Chiefs. It would be another six months before they could report to training camp and put the stench of the Super Bowl behind them.

"All winter, all spring, all offseason all we got to hear was how lousy of a league we are, how lousy of a team we are," Arbanas said. "We took about as much criticism as we could possibly take."

That offseason the Chiefs received their rings for winning the AFL championship. Buck Buchanan never wore his.

The players may have been looking toward July to redeem themselves. But Stram and his staff of coaches and scouts were looking toward March. The AFL and NFL would stage their first common draft then. The bidding war was over. When you draft a player, he's yours. There would be no more draft picks like Bob Lilly, Roger Staubach, Gale Sayers, and Mike Curtis who could reject the Chiefs and sign with the other league.

So Kansas City's hunt for better defenders would start in March. But first, there was one last bit of unfinished business from 1966 to address.

Jan Stenerud 27

Jan Stenerud was a last vestige of the AFL-NFL signing wars.

By 1966 the two leagues were conducting redshirt drafts, selecting players with college eligibility remaining just to secure future negotiation rights. The expansion Atlanta Falcons claimed Stenerud with the first overall pick of the NFL redshirt draft, and the Kansas City Chiefs took him in the third round of the AFL draft.

The fact that Stenerud was even on the radar of professional football in 1966 was remarkable.

Stenerud was from Norway. He came to the United States on a ski jumping scholarship from Montana State and became an All-American in that sport for the Bobcats. Which explained his presence at the school's football stadium in the fall of 1964.

"I used to run around the stadium track almost every day in the fall to get my legs in shape for the ski jump season," Stenerud said. "One day some of the kids were out there kicking footballs. I knew some of them, so I joined in. I thought to myself, 'Gosh, I haven't kicked a ball for years.' So I went out with tennis shoes on and kicked extra points with the toe like everyone else. I didn't do very well, so I thought to myself, 'There has to be a better way of doing this.' So I lined up like I was going to take a corner kick or a penalty kick in soccer. I got the ball airborne, end-over-end, and it went pretty well."

Montana State basketball coach Roger Craft happened to be in the stadium that day, and the thunderous sound of ball hitting Stenerud's foot caught his attention. So did the distance of his kick.

"He came walking across the field and said, 'Do that again,'" Stenerud said. "He moved me out for some long ones, and I kicked them pretty good. He went running over to the football coach, Jim Sweeney, and said,

'There's a Norwegian skier out there kicking the hell out of the football.' Of course, Sweeney had heard kicker stories before, and he didn't pay too much attention to it."

But later that fall, Stenerud was running the steps of the stadium as the Bobcats were preparing for their Camellia Bowl game.

"Hey, Stenerud," Sweeney barked, "I hear you can kick. Get down here."

Stenerud didn't realize it at the time, but this was his tryout.

"I had on tennis shoes," Stenerud said. "[Sweeney] was wearing football cleats, so he took them off and said, 'Put these on.' He asked me if I could kick off, and I honestly didn't know for sure what a kickoff was. I had gone to the games, but I didn't pay much attention because I thought football was such a boring game. I understood basketball better.

"Well, I kicked off a few for him, and one of them went through the goalposts. They had never seen anything like that. I didn't know how good that was. Some of the guys out there said there was a guy they had seen on television, Pete Gogolak, who was making a living kicking the football like that. They told me I ought to go out for the team."

So Stenerud went out for the team in 1965 and became the placekicker in a season to forget as the Bobcats finished 3–7. But Stenerud did something unforgettable that season: kicking a 59-yard field goal against Montana. It was the longest field goal at the time by either a professional or college kicker.

But that wasn't his most memorable kick of his college career.

"I tried a 112-yard field goal," Stenerud said. "Remember that the rules were different back then. The ball didn't come back to the spot of the miss. Well, the wind was blowing 90 miles an hour and our punter was terrible. So we're on our 5-yard line, and I'm lining up two yards deep in our end zone. I'm standing on my tippy-toes trying to see where the goalposts are, and all of a sudden I realize, 'Why in the world am I looking for the goalposts? Don't waste your time—Just get the darn thing out of there.'"

The Chiefs began their pitch wooing Stenerud away from the Falcons and the NFL on December 11, 1966, flying him to Miami for their game with the Dolphins. Smart move—out of the cold of Montana and into the warmth of Florida. Stenerud signed with the Chiefs on December 20, 1966, two days after Kansas City finished the 1966 regular season.

The scout who signed Stenerud was Bobby Beathard, who would later be enshrined in the Pro Football Hall of Fame for his prowess in team-building as a general manager.

Stenerud was assigned a third-story room in the dormitory at William Jewell College for his first AFL training camp that July. He remembers lugging his portable black-and-white television set up three flights of stairs back in the day when TVs were anything but portable.

"It turns out the Hammer (Fred Williamson) had the room next to mine," Stenerud said. "He said, 'Hey, rook—what are you bringing that TV up for? You're going to be gone in three days."

Although now a professional football player, Stenerud was still in just his third year of organized football. There was so much for him to learn about the sport. And two of the lessons came in his first game with the Chiefs—the exhibition opener against the Houston Oilers at Rice Stadium.

"Rice Stadium had two sets of goalposts," Lamar Hunt said. "The college goalposts were set in concrete on the (back) goal line, and they put up some temporary (pro) posts on the goal line. Jan came out and said, 'What's this?' and Johnny Robinson told him, 'This is pro football. If you kick it through one you get three points, and if you kick it through both you get six points.' Jan fell for it a little bit."

The second lesson wasn't verbal. It was physical. The Chiefs called a fair catch at midfield on a punt at the end of the first half, giving them the option of a free kick. They could attempt a field goal try from the point of the catch with no rush from the Oilers.

"All of a sudden Hank said, 'Kickoff team . . . Dawson stays and he'll hold,'" Stenerud explained. "I didn't have any idea what was going on, but I realized that since I was out there I might as well aim for the goalposts. It was about a 55-yarder, and I pulled it left. As we were running off the field, I asked Lenny, 'What was that?' I haven't seen one since."

Stenerud was all the Chiefs hoped he'd be in his first season, leading the league with twenty-one field goals and also kicking the longest field goal of the AFL season, a 54-yarder. He scored 100 points in each of his first five seasons and went to two AFL All-Star Games and two Pro Bowls.

"In those days it wasn't common knowledge what other players were making," Stenerud said. "But somehow I found out that Pete Gogolak was making more money than I was. He was asking $33,000, and I was asking $30,000. I had a better year than Pete, and I felt I should make more money. I told Hank that.

"While I was in his office, he said he'd call the general manager of the Giants. So he gets on the phone and says, 'Stenerud's in my office here and says Gogolak is making $33,000. That isn't right is it? He's making $26,000, isn't it? Yeah, I thought so.'

"I'm sitting on the coach 15 feet away, and I never hear the other end of the conversation. So Hank hangs up and says, 'Naw, Gogolak isn't making $33,000, he's making $26,000.' I long accused him of calling his own secretary down the hall instead of the general manager of the Giants. He just laughed."

"I did call the Giants that time," Stram contended. *That time . . .*

Mike Mercer started the 1966 season in Oakland, but after converting only one of four field goal tries, the Raiders cut him. The Bills then signed Mercer as an insurance policy for their own kicker, Booth Lusteg. But a month into the season, the Chiefs lost kicker Tommy Brooker with an injury.

So the Bills loaned Mercer to the Chiefs, and he proved pivotal in their success, kicking an AFL-leading twenty-one field goals in thirty attempts. He returned to Buffalo in 1967, and Stenerud proved a worthy replacement. For the next eleven seasons the Chiefs would enjoy the most stable kicking situation in all of football with Stenerud and punter Jerrel Wilson.

Willie Lanier 28

The rebuilding of the Kansas City defense was off to a rocky start.

The Chiefs used their first three selections in the 1967 draft on defenders: Miami end Gene Trosch with the 24th pick of the first round, then two middle linebackers in the second round—Notre Dame's Jim Lynch with the 47th pick and Morgan State's Willie Lanier with the 50th pick.

A week later the Chiefs sent Lloyd Wells, their African American scout, to visit Lanier at Morgan State with a contract offer—a signing bonus of $2,500 and a three-year contract for the AFL minimum of $14,000 the first year, $15,000 the second, and $16,000 the third. Then Wells said something that stunned Lanier.

"If you don't take what we're offering, you can take your *motherfucking* ass to Canada to play football," Wells told the young linebacker.

The Chiefs may have thought they knew Willie Lanier the player, but they certainly didn't know Willie Lanier the person.

Lanier didn't start playing football until his junior year in high school and didn't play linebacker until his senior year. He had one scholarship offer and it was from an HBCU school in his home state, Virginia State. But Lanier wanted to play his football north of the Mason-Dixon Line. A high school teammate, quarterback Gilbert Carter, received a scholarship from Morgan State in Baltimore, so after graduation in June, Lanier called coach Earl Banks and said he wanted to attend school and play football there.

"Son, I don't know a thing about you," Banks said.

"What do you need to know?" Lanier asked.

Transcripts and game films, Banks told him. So unbeknownst even to his parents or his football coaches, Lanier returned to Walker High School in Richmond after graduation and arranged for the transcripts and films to be sent to Banks. Both viewings intrigued the Morgan State coach.

"He told me I was welcome to come but that he had already expended all of his budget (scholarship money) for the freshman class," Lanier recalled. "He also told me I'd have to take an entrance examination."

No problem—Lanier took the test and scored among the top 10 percent of the school's incoming freshman class.

"I don't have any (scholarship) money to offer you," Banks said.

"I'm not asking for money," Lanier told him. "I want to go to your school, and whatever my parents and I have to do, we'll do. You'll be impressed with my academic and athletic work, and whatever you need to do you'll do in the future."

Lanier started at nose tackle as a walk-on freshman but moved to middle linebacker as a sophomore on scholarship. He became a small-college All-American in both his junior and senior seasons. Morgan State went undefeated both years, and Lanier was the MVP of the Tangerine Bowl in his final college game. He also was earning a degree in his four years on campus in business. Lanier traveled to Washington D.C. as a senior to research his senior-class paper on the "Monopolistic Aspects of Professional Football."

Lanier also had a friend in a high place. Buddy Young was a Pro Bowl running back for the Baltimore Colts in the 1950s, and he had also been a high school teammate of Banks. In 1966, he was an executive who worked for the NFL in New York. He was spreading the word in his circles about a talented linebacker at Morgan State. It turns out Wells was one of the listeners. Young also had some valuable information to share with Lanier—the details of the contract offered to Jim Lynch by the Chiefs: a $40,000 signing bonus with salaries of $20,000 in each of the three years of the deal.

So the threat from Wells did not sit well with Lanier. There was quite a disparity between what the Chiefs offered their white All-American middle linebacker from Notre Dame and their Black All-American middle linebacker from Morgan State drafted just three picks later. Lanier wondered if the Chiefs told Lynch he could take his *motherfucking* ass to Canada in their negotiations.

"That was my introduction to the National Football League," Lanier said. "Nobody had ever used that language toward me previously. I told [Wells] three things would happen. First, I would not go to Canada to play football. Two, you need to go back to Kansas City and tell them they sent the wrong son-of-a-bitch to see me. And three, I will sue you all."

The next day Lanier called Kansas City coach Hank Stram.

"I told him, 'Let me explain something to you. I'm a graduating senior at Morgan State College, and if you think you can send someone to disrespect me, you're wrong. The draft you had means nothing to me. I may never even play pro football. I may never come to Kansas City. But you will not disrespect me,'" Lanier said. "Then I tried to break the phone when I hung up."

Lanier did not participate in any offseason activities with the Chiefs that spring and was prepared to walk away from football. He had a business degree and his dignity. But Stram got involved and handled the contract negotiations himself. Lanier eventually settled on a one-year contract for $18,000 with a $25,000 signing bonus.

Both Lanier and Lynch were invited to play in the College All-Star Game that summer against the Green Bay Packers. Lynch went, but Lanier did not. His college coach Earl Banks never told him of the invitation.

"He said he felt it made more sense at that point in time that I needed to get to camp and get started on the work that needed to be done," Lanier said.

Wise man. Only one other African American (Garland Boyette) had ever started an NFL game at middle linebacker, but he wound up in Canada after only six starts in 1962 with the St. Louis Cardinals. So Lanier did indeed have some work to do.

During the two weeks Lynch spent with the College All-Stars, Lanier was showing the Chiefs the size, speed, and ability at middle linebacker that they would need to compete with NFL teams.

"When Jim came back from the All-Star Game, they never moved Willie," Kansas City cornerback Emmitt Thomas recalled. "They moved Jim."

That was testimony to Stram and his even-handedness in building both a roster and a starting lineup.

"I told people it didn't make any difference to me whether you were Black or white or polka-dot or Catholic or Polish," Stram said. "It didn't make any difference to me whether they were All-Americas, where they played or what they did. You had to earn the right to play. The players felt strongly about that. I don't think they ever felt that anybody walked in and became a player and a winner just because of what he did in college.

"The greatest endorsement of that was when we had Willie Lanier and Jim Lynch. I knew from the first time they lined up that Lanier was going to be a better middle linebacker than Lynch. There wasn't a Black middle linebacker at that time, and the players were saying, 'Now we'll see.' You can't fool players. They knew right off the bat that Lanier should be the middle linebacker. When that decision was made, it solidified what our whole team was all about."

Stram was putting the pieces in place for a bigger, faster, more physical defense—and younger. End Aaron Brown (six-five, 255 pounds) had been a first-round draft pick in 1966, and Emmitt Thomas (six-two, 192) signed as an undrafted college free agent. Both spent their rookie seasons as reserves. Trosch, Lanier, and Lynch all arrived in 1967.

But Stram was reluctant to commit to all that youth. Any of it, in fact. When the 1967 season started, the cast of the starting defense was the same as what lined up in the Super Bowl. Before season's end, though, Thomas would replace Fred Williamson at left cornerback, Lanier would replace Sherrill Headrick at middle linebacker, and Lynch would replace E. J. Holub at weakside linebacker. Lanier started nine games as a rookie, Thomas six, and Lynch five.

But Lanier's career almost ended before it could begin. And he almost lost more than his career—his *life*.

In a game against San Diego in his rookie season, Lanier dove over the block of a pulling guard to make a tackle. But while he was airborne, the knee of the ball carrier clipped the front of Lanier's helmet. He finished the game with no issues, but the following week Lanier collapsed on the field. It turns out he had suffered a subdural hematoma against the Chargers that caused internal bleeding in his brain that built up over the week and caused him to black out that Sunday.

"Years later the team doctor told me they lost my pulse three times," Lanier said. "I almost died."

Lanier went to the Mayo Clinic for the diagnosis. Afterward, equipment manager Bobby Yarborough added a thick pad to the top of his helmet's exterior to add further protection for his head. But Lanier didn't need it.

He already determined what he needed to do to continue playing football and have a quality of life afterward.

"I didn't really use my head anymore," Lanier said. "I had to remove all those impacts, so I took my head completely out of the game after my first year. I managed it so that the head never touched anybody in practice or games. I didn't miss but five minutes of a game in the next ten years."

His nickname became "Contact" for the physicality of his hits. One St. Louis writer even dubbed him "the Black Butkus."

"I was somewhat offended by it," Lanier said. "My point was that they didn't call Butkus the white Willie Lanier."

Lanier would get the chance to see Butkus up close in August of his rookie year.

The Chicago Bears 29

Gale Sayers was born in Wichita and played his college football at the University of Kansas with great fanfare. He earned All-Big Eight acclaim three times and All-American honors twice.

Sayers became known as "The Kansas Comet" during his college days in Lawrence.

The Kansas City Chiefs were anxious to keep Sayers home for his professional football career. When his franchise played in Dallas, owner Lamar Hunt saw the value of adding familiar names and faces to his roster to attract fans, so he loaded up on talented Texans. Now that his franchise was playing in Kansas City, Hunt saw the same value in adding Sayers to the Chiefs.

So Kansas City invested the fifth overall choice of the 1965 AFL draft on the Kansas Comet. But the Chicago Bears chose Sayers with the fourth overall pick of the NFL draft. His decision would come down to the stability of the NFL versus the bankroll of the AFL. The stability won out.

Sayers was part of the greatest first round by a team in NFL history. The Bears claimed Dick Butkus and Sayers on back-to-back selections, the third and fourth overall choices of the 1965 draft. The Denver Broncos drafted Butkus with the ninth overall pick of the AFL draft, but he also opted for the stability of the NFL. Sayers set a record with twenty-two touchdowns that season and was named the NFL's Rookie of the Year. Butkus joined Sayers as a first-team All-Pro and finished second in the Rookie of the Year voting.

A Kansas City franchise without a dynamic Sayers failed miserably in the first Super Bowl, and the postgame comments were biting.

"The press was badgering (Vince) Lombardi to make comparisons," Len Dawson said. "He tried not to answer it . . . but finally he said there were other teams in the NFL who could beat the Chiefs, including teams in their own division like the Bears. And look who we had coming up in that preseason—the Bears."

As part of the merger agreement, the two leagues would play a championship game in 1966 and then an annual series of exhibition games starting in the summer of 1967. The first matchup on the second weekend of the preseason sent the NFL Detroit Lions to Denver to play the AFL Broncos. Denver lost its exhibition opener to the worst team in the AFL, the expansion Dolphins, and Detroit's Hall of Fame defensive tackle Alex Karras said he'd walk home if the Lions lost to the AFL team. The Broncos won, 13–7 . . . and Karras flew home with the team.

Johnny Unitas and the Baltimore Colts visited Boston in week two and dismantled the Patriots, 33–3. The Philadelphia Eagles traveled to Cincinnati in week three for a neutral field game against Joe Namath and the New York Jets and prevailed, 34–19. The Bears were sent to Kansas City in week four to dispatch of the defending AFL champion Chiefs.

"We wanted them because of what happened in the Super Bowl," Dawson said. "We got kicked. We played the Packers close for a half and then got blown out in the second half. We had to live with that for six or seven months. Had the Super Bowl been close, that Bear game wouldn't have meant anything. But the Packers had beaten us badly."

It certainly meant something to Kansas City coach Hank Stram.

"I got a copy of the Super Bowl highlight film and showed it to the team on the day of the game," Stram said. "There was a great displeasure on the part of our players about the way the film was done, the way it downplayed our team and our league. There were enough things said to infuriate our football team. We felt determined to make amends. So our motivation was high."

The Chiefs won their first three exhibition games against AFL competition, routing the Oilers 24–9, the Jets 30–17, and the Raiders 48–0. But Kansas City had come to expect winning in August. Those three victories extended the Chiefs' preseason winning streak to nine games. But that streak figured to face its stiffest challenge against an NFL opponent the caliber of the Bears.

"The Bears came in here thinking this was an exhibition game," Dawson said. "This wasn't a preseason game—it was an opportunity for us to redeem ourselves. In the preseason you normally put in things week after week so that by the end of camp, your playbook was complete. But, brother, it was already all in for the Bears. Because we were such a veteran team, our playbook was mid-season when the Bears came in here."

There was nothing vanilla about the Kansas City game plan in this otherwise meaningless exhibition game. The innovative Stram was doing things on offense in the AFL that NFL teams had never seen before. And he was going to take full advantage of that lack of familiarity by the Bears.

"The Bears had never played against our tight I formation," Stram said. "Back then the Bears used a strongside linebacker and a weakside linebacker, a strongside tackle and a weakside tackle, a strongside safety and a weakside safety. It all depended on which side the tight end lined up."

Stram's tight I had tight end Fred Arbanas lined up in the backfield, and he would motion out before the snap.

"So when we shifted Freddie out of the backfield, they'd move six people to our one," Stram said. "Sometimes they'd be standing back there waiting for the tight end to shift, and we'd run a quick count on them with Freddie still back there. We had a lot of fun with it."

The Chiefs didn't have Sayers but they did have Mike Garrett, who won a Heisman Trophy at Southern Cal. And Stram was going to make sure he was ready to run against the Bears.

"Hank asked me, 'How do you like your field?'" Garrett said. "I said, 'I like it cut short. I like a track meet. If I have my quickness, I can play with anybody.' (Groundskeeper George) Toma came over before the Bears game and asked me, 'Is this what you want?' I said, 'It's perfect. It's a speed track.' I loved Municipal."

It was a perfect evening for football in Kansas City with clear skies, a slight breeze, and a temperature in the 80s. It was the only home exhibition game of the summer for the Chiefs, but a less-than-sellout crowd of 33,041 turned out on a Wednesday night for the city's first ever glimpse of an NFL team. The last time the Chiefs were at home in November, a crowd of 41,475 turned out to see them play the Boston Patriots on the road to the Super Bowl.

The game started off innocently enough. The Bears won the toss, and a touchback gave them possession at the Kansas City 20. As if to remind Hunt, the Chiefs, and their fans what they were missing, Chicago handed the ball to Sayers on each of the first two plays. He went up the middle for 2 yards on first down and around left end for 3 yards on second down. The Bears would drive 52 yards in eight plays, setting up a 35-yard Mike Alford field goal and a 3–0 lead.

The Chiefs punted on their first two possessions, gaining only 8 yards in their six offensive snaps. The home crowd was starting to get antsy. Could the Chiefs play with these NFL teams or not?

The answer came at the end of the first quarter. Starting Kansas City's third possession at his own 17, Dawson went to the air, and the Bears were penalized 13 yards for pass interference on a toss to Curtis McClinton, another Kansas back not known as the Comet. Then Dawson completed a 70-yard touchdown pass to Otis Taylor on the final play of the quarter for a 7–3 lead.

E. J. Holub intercepted a Rudy Bukich pass on the first play of the second quarter and returned it to the Chicago 11. Dawson hit Chris Burford on the next play for a touchdown. The Chiefs touched the ball four more times in the second quarter and scored three more touchdowns plus a Jan Stenerud field goal. Garrett rushed for one score, and Dawson threw passes to Gloster Richardson and Taylor for the other two. That put the Chiefs up 39–10 at halftime.

The two teams traded touchdowns in the third quarter and it was 46–17 after forty-five minutes.

"We were up two or three touchdowns in the third quarter, and I'm coming back from a deep route, and [Bears safety] Richie Petitbon says to me, 'Chris, when are you guys going to lay off?'" Burford said. "And I said, 'It won't be tonight, Richie, it won't be tonight.'

"We just said screw these guys and kept pouring it on. We played our starters a little longer than usual for a blowout. We had taken so much verbal abuse from the media—magazines, television networks, newspapers—the whole offseason. It was a very exciting game. The atmosphere was the most electric I've ever been around in sports. The fans went nuts."

The Chiefs had a horse mascot named Warpaint that would gallop around the football field after every Kansas City score. In the third quarter, Butkus warned Dawson, "You'd better stop scoring or you're going to kill that horse."

Chicago coach George Halas went to his backups in the third quarter, but Stram waited until the fourth quarter to empty his bench. Pete Beathard replaced Dawson at quarterback, and Kansas City's two rookie linebackers—Willie Lanier and Jim Lynch—finally hit the field. But that didn't slow the Chiefs any.

Beathard passed for one touchdown, ran for another, and Noland "Super Gnat" Smith returned a kickoff 99 yards for a score. The final points came on a Beathard bootleg with forty-one seconds left in the game. The Chiefs attempted a 2-point conversion to push the count to 68 but failed.

"It was fun running it up," Dawson said. "Fred Arbanas was on the sideline, and when we got to 66 points, he said, 'Let's go for 100.' That proved to us we could play with the big boys."

Game balls were handed out to four members of the franchise—the four men who were haunted most by the Super Bowl loss to the Packers: Hunt, Stram, Dawson, and Mitchell.

Kansas City's players earned the respect of the Bears but not their style.

"They were a good football team, make no mistake about that," said Petitbon, Chicago's Pro Bowl safety. "They probably had better athletes than we gave them credit for. And they ran it up. Back in those days the leagues were at war, and it was just one of those things. We never had a chance to get back at them. You can do something like that to another team, especially if you know you're not going to play them again in the near future. I think they would have been reluctant to run it up if we had them home-and-home. They took their shot."

The Chiefs were indeed in midseason form, gaining 474 yards with twenty-six first downs against the Butkus-led defense. The Chiefs rushed for 182 yards and did not commit any turnovers. Taylor caught four passes for 130 yards and those two scores and also took an end-around for another 32 yards. Sayers rushed for only 35 yards in ten carries, and the Bears committed four turnovers, which the Chiefs converted into 24 points.

"That was one of the fun games I can ever remember," Burford said. "You had to be there to really experience it. I was doing television sports on the side at the time with the NBC station in Kansas City. So I got a lot of the teletype that came into the station. After that game I went up to the station and read some of it. When it was 29–3, there was a message—

'Please send back the corrected score.' They figured we couldn't possibly be ahead."

After the game, Chicago offensive line coach Abe Gibron charged after Stram. The two had been college teammates at Purdue.

Stram said, "Abe shook his fist and said, 'Do you realize you embarrassed a legend?' We weren't trying to embarrass anyone. We were just trying to win the game. Even though it wasn't a league game, it was still a game. Every game we played, we played with the idea of winning. It was just one of those games when everything we did was like you'd draw it up on paper. Everything we did was perfect. We probably couldn't do that again in another 100 years."

Speaking of a hundred years, the Bears have been playing football for more than a century. Those 66 points were the most ever scored against them in any game—preseason, regular season, or postseason.

"I was born and raised in Chicago," Stram explained. "I grew up in the shadows of Wrigley Field. The Bears were always my team as I was growing up. I had an emotional tie to them. I'd sneak off and watch them practice whenever I could. When I was coaching at Purdue we used to go over to Rensselaer to see them in training. I had a great respect for George Halas.

"It's funny though. We played the Bears five times when I was the coach of the Chiefs and the Saints, and we won all five games."

But this was the most important game Stram would ever play against the Bears. The Chiefs claimed their redemption.

"It was the most fascinating game I have ever experienced," Stenerud said. "The whole town was on fire. The stadium rocked for three hours. I can remember the satisfaction it gave the older guys like Arbanas, Mays, Dawson, Buchanan, and Robinson. I thought if every game in the NFL is going to be like this, it's going to be a wild ride."

But it wouldn't be.

The Long Road Back 30

Every team that ever reaches a championship game expects to return the following season. If you've been the best in your conference or league once, you believe you can do it again.

That's what Joe Schmidt and the 1958 Detroit Lions believed. That's what Joe Namath and the 1969 New York Jets, Dan Marino and the 1985 Miami Dolphins, and Larry Fitzgerald and the 2009 Arizona Cardinals all believed. But those legendary players and their franchises never played for another NFL championship.

Len Dawson and the 1967 Kansas City Chiefs believed they would return to the Super Bowl as well. They saw the Green Bay Packers in the first Super Bowl and found them to be human. They played a team that summer that carried the NFL flag as the league's charter franchise and humiliated the Chicago Bears.

The 1967 Chiefs believed they were an older, wiser, and better team than the squad that represented the AFL in the first Super Bowl. Jan Stenerud gave Hank Stram a dynamic new weapon with his leg, both on kickoffs and field goals. Kansas City's top three draft picks infused size, speed, and youth into the defensive front, addressing a weakness that was exposed by the Packers.

So the Chiefs were anxious to return to the second Super Bowl and wouldn't mind playing the Packers again. But Kansas City wasn't the only AFL team that believed it was markedly better in 1967 than in 1966. The Houston Oilers and Oakland Raiders were also anxious to start up again.

The Oilers finished a franchise-worst 3–11 in 1966 in Wally Lemm's first season as head coach. At thirty-nine, George Blanda was no longer playing like an AFL MVP, so the Oilers released him that offseason. Houston drafted All-American linebacker George Webster of Michigan

State with the fifth overall pick of the 1967 draft, and they also acquired veteran cornerback Miller Farr in a trade with the San Diego Chargers.

The Raiders finished 8-5-1 in 1966 in John Rauch's first season as head coach. Oakland drafted guard Gene Upshaw with its first-round pick and made two key trades, acquiring quarterback Daryle "The Mad Bomber" Lamonica from the Buffalo Bills and cornerback Willie Brown from the Denver Broncos. Oakland also signed Blanda to handle its placekicking and back up Lamonica.

Because the Chiefs shared Municipal Stadium with the baseball A's, they spent most of their September Sundays on the road. The 1967 season would be no different. For the third consecutive fall and fourth time in their five years in Kansas City, the Chiefs opened the season with a three-game road trip. The first two games were no problem—Kansas City toppled a Houston team still trying to figure out its quarterback position in the opener, 25–20, then whipped the Miami Dolphins, 24–0.

But the third weekend meant a trip to Oakland, which also meant trouble. Lamonica threw a pair of touchdown passes, and Blanda kicked three field goals to give the Raiders a 23–21 victory. The Chiefs walloped the Dolphins again in the fourth weekend, 41–0, and the Raiders fell to the Jets in New York. That left Kansas City and Oakland tied for the AFL West with a 3–1 record.

Looking to bulk up their defensive line, the Chiefs traded their backup quarterback Pete Beathard to the Oilers for Ernie "Big Cat" Ladd the first week of October. That gave Kansas City the biggest set of tackles in pro football with the six-nine, 290-pound Ladd and the six-seven, 287-pound Buchanan. But it also gave the Oilers the answer to their quarterbacking woes.

The Chiefs dropped their next two games to San Diego and Houston to fall to .500. In his first start for the Oilers, Beathard threw a touchdown pass in the 24–19 victory over Kansas City. He would start the final nine games of the season for Houston and win seven of them, lifting the Oilers to their first Eastern Division title since 1962. Houston finished 9-4-1.

At 3–3, the Chiefs believed they could still make up ground on the 5–1 Raiders in the West. But Oakland wouldn't let them. The Raiders won their final ten games of the season to finish 13–1, then demolished the

Oilers in the AFL title game, 40–7, for the right to play the Packers in the second Super Bowl.

The Chiefs went 5–1 against the West on the way to the Super Bowl in 1966 but went 2–4 in the division in 1967 with a pair of losses to both Oakland and San Diego.

The highlight was also a lowlight. The AFL created a Thanksgiving Day game that season to compete with the NFL games in Dallas and Detroit, and Kansas City was designated as the permanent host. A crowd of forty-four thousand turned out to see the rematch with the Raiders on Thanksgiving, but the Chiefs suffered their worst loss since the Super Bowl, a 44–22 trouncing. Dawson threw four interceptions, and the Raiders returned two of them for touchdowns, including one by Willie Brown.

Lamonica passed for thirty touchdowns and rushed for four more in capturing AFL MVP honors. Blanda led the AFL in scoring with 116 points, and Hall of Famer Fred Biletnikoff went to his first AFL All-Star Game after averaging 21.9 yards per catch. But the Raiders, like the Chiefs, proved no match for the Packers, losing 33–14 in the second Super Bowl.

Webster was named the AFL Rookie of the Year and made first-team All-Pro in each of his first three seasons. Farr led the AFL with ten interceptions in 1967 and was voted first-team All-Pro in each of his first two seasons. Hoyle Granger rushed for 1,194 yards and led the AFL with 1,494 yards from scrimmage to join Webster and Farr at the league's All-Star Game.

On the East Coast, Joe Namath became the first quarterback in pro football history to pass for 4,000 yards in a single season for the 8-5-1 New York Jets in 1967. On the West Coast, John Hadl was warming up in San Diego, throwing ten touchdown passes to his All-Star tight end Willie Frazier and eight more to his All-Star flanker Lance Alworth for the 8-5-1 Chargers.

And suddenly the Super Bowl was no longer a foregone conclusion for the Chiefs.

So Hank Stram did not stand pat in 1968 as he attempted to do in 1967. He no longer had that luxury. His Chiefs lost longtime starters Chris Burford, Sherrill Headrick, and Bobby Hunt to the Cincinnati Bengals in the expansion draft. So Stram did some shuffling.

Frank Pitts replaced Burford, first-round draft pick Mo Moorman took over for Curt Merz at right guard, and Holub moved from linebacker to center. But not by choice. Holub went to five AFL All-Star Games as a linebacker and wanted to stay there. Unfortunately injuries had taken a toll on his body.

"E.J.'s knees would not allow him to play linebacker the way he wanted or the way we wanted him to play it anymore," Stram said. "He couldn't stay at linebacker, but guys like E.J. are a special breed. He was like a perpetual rookie, and you've got to find a way to keep those guys around. He didn't want to play center, but I had to convince him it was in the best interest of the team. We had a big offensive line, and we needed a big center in the middle of it. I wanted E.J. in there, and it would extend his career."

Fourteenth-round draft pick Robert Holmes surprisingly won a starting spot and led the Chiefs in rushing with 866 yards. Over on defense, Aaron Brown finally moved into the starting lineup at right end, Willie Lanier and Jim Lynch became entrenched at linebacker, and Jim Kearney took over at safety for Hunt.

There was another key addition. The Denver Broncos drafted Arizona State defensive tackle Curley Culp in the second round of the 1968 draft. He measured six-two, 265 pounds, and the Broncos thought he was too short to play defensive tackle. Denver tried him at guard but wasn't happy with the results. So during training camp the Broncos dealt Culp to the Chiefs for a fourth-round draft pick.

Culp was a former NCAA heavyweight wrestling champion. The Chiefs loved his hand and foot speed plus a low center of gravity that gained him leverage on blockers. But Culp played sparingly as a rookie behind the three veteran defensive tackles already on the roster—Buchanan, Ladd, and Ed Lothamer.

The A's left for Oakland in 1968, so the Chiefs were finally able to play two of their first three games at home. Except Namath came to Kansas City on the second week of the season and passed for 302 yards and a pair of touchdowns in a 20–19 victory by the Jets. Kansas City allowed 41 points in the first two games of the season, finding itself 1–1 and again chasing the 2–0 Raiders.

At that point, the Chiefs defensively turned off the tap. Kansas City held its next four opponents to single-digit scoring, then held nine of its last twelve foes to 10 points or less. A great defense was materializing. The Chiefs suffered only one more loss the rest of the season, a 38–21 dismantling by the Raiders in Oakland in November. Two weekends earlier, Kansas City defeated Oakland at home, 24–10.

The Raiders lost another game that season to the Chargers, leaving Oakland and Kansas City deadlocked for first place in the West at season's end with 12–2 records. That set up a divisional playoff game in Oakland between the highest-scoring offense in the AFL—the Raiders with 453 points—and the league's stingiest defense—the Chiefs, who allowed only 170 points.

It was no contest. Lamonica threw three touchdown passes in the first quarter to put the Raiders up 21–0 on the way to a 41–6 victory. No excuses.

"They were better," Lanier said. "They just did a better job that day than we did."

But this time the Raiders were denied a return trip to the Super Bowl. Namath threw three touchdown passes at home for a 27–23 victory over the Raiders in the AFL championship game. Now it was the Jets' chance to accomplish what the Chiefs and Raiders had failed to do—defeat the NFL champion in a Super Bowl. And the Jets did just that, upsetting the Baltimore Colts, 16–7.

Coming off a 12–2 season, Stram knew he had an offense that was Super Bowl-ready. But he knew the Jets and Raiders had teams that were just as capable. The Chiefs still had some tinkering to do on the defense, and step one was to draft bump-and-run cornerback Jim Marsalis of Tennessee State in the first round.

Kansas City had six players from the AFL's best defense invited to the 1968 AFL All-Star Game. Marsalis gave them potentially a seventh such All-Star for 1969. It would be the Kansas City defense against the mighty offenses of the Raiders and Jets for the right to play in the fourth Super Bowl.

Step two was to promote Culp to the starting lineup. His speed provided a dynamic complement to the size of five-time AFL All-Star Buchanan on his left and six-time All-Star Jerry Mays on his right.

"With Curley we were able to play either a three-four [defensive front] or a four-three based on the center and the offense that you played," Lanier said. "Having Curley inside and (Aaron) Brown on the edge, it became a different game. As big as they were, offenses couldn't block either one of them with one person. We could create mismatches that caused all kinds of problems."

As was the case when Kansas City last won the AFL in 1966, the Chiefs went undefeated during the preseason, posting a 6–0 record with four of the victories against NFL teams. Kansas City was now 7–2 against NFL competition since the Super Bowl loss to the Packers.

But even with the A's in Oakland now, the Chiefs faced their most daunting season-opening schedule—four consecutive road games from coast to coast. They opened in San Diego, then flew to Boston, followed by trips to Cincinnati and Denver. Kansas City's only loss was a surprising 24–19 setback to the second-year Bengals.

But the Chiefs suffered an even bigger loss in the second week when Dawson left the Boston game with a potential season-ending knee injury. Jacky Lee started in his place in the third week against the Bengals, but after throwing for only 78 yards, he left the game with a leg injury. That forced Stram to turn his offense over to inexperienced Mike Livingston. He appeared in only one game in his rookie season in 1968 and didn't throw his first AFL pass until the second half of the 1969 Cincinnati game.

And suddenly Kansas City's Super Bowl hopes seemed hopeless.

But Kansas City's defense stepped up, building a wall at the goal line in holding five of the next six opponents to 13 points or less. Dawson made it back to the field sooner than expected, missing only five games, and Livingston won all five of his starts to keep the Chiefs afloat in the West. Livingston threw for 308 yards in the victory over Miami and three touchdowns in a home rematch with the Bengals.

Dawson won his first two starts back, including a 34–16 romp over the Jets in New York, to extend Kansas City's winning streak to seven games. That set up a showdown with the Raiders in Kansas City in week eleven. The Chiefs were 9–1, the Raiders 8-1-1.

But as was the case in that Thanksgiving game of 1967, errant throws by Dawson sank the Chiefs. He threw five interceptions, and, again, two were returned for touchdowns, allowing the Raiders to prevail, 27–24.

In the rematch against the Raiders three weeks later in Oakland, the Chiefs again came up short, losing 10–6. Dawson threw only six passes and completed two of them.

That left the Chiefs as a second-place finisher at 11–3, trailing the 12-1-1 Raiders. Which meant Kansas City would have to win back-to-back road playoff games if it hoped to return to the Super Bowl. The Chiefs would have to go on the road and beat the 1968 AFL champion Jets in the first game and likely the 1967 AFL champion Raiders in the second.

First up, the defending Super Bowl champion Jets. And Joe Namath.

"We loved playing against Joe," linebacker Bobby Bell said. "That's how you blossom—playing against the best brings out your best."

And Namath certainly brought out the best in the Chiefs. They had already beaten him in New York that season, intercepting Namath three times in a 34–16 victory in November. The Chiefs played Namath four times in his career in New York and beat him all four times. Overall, Kansas City was 5–2 against Namath with more interceptions (ten) than he had thrown touchdown passes (nine).

But this was the latest the Chiefs had ever played the Jets, and the weather was going to be a factor. The game-time temperature was 33°F and falling, with a wind chill of 22°F. There also was an 18 mile-per-hour wind gusting through Shea Stadium. That created havoc in the downfield passing lanes for both quarterbacks, minimizing the impact of the three All-Star receivers in the game—Otis Taylor, Don Maynard, and George Sauer.

Short passes and short runs became the order of the day. Only three AFL teams scored 300 points in the 1969 AFL season, and the Chiefs and Jets were two of them. But through forty-five minutes, the two offenses could only manage three field goals—and Kansas City carried a 6–3 lead into the fourth quarter.

The Chiefs were penalized twice on New York's next possession—15 yards for roughing the passer and 18 yards for pass interference on Emmitt Thomas in the end zone—giving the Jets possession at the Kansas City 1. Namath was faced with a first-and-goal with a chance to take the lead. Lanier was irate.

"It was understood that if they scored a touchdown, you'd put yourself in a hole you might not be able to get out of," Lanier said. "So I started raising hell (in the huddle) about who they were and how we had to fight from training camp to [get] where we were and that we were not going to let them score. But I knew that words without action weren't going to mean anything."

With the largest crowd ever—62,977—to see an AFL game on its feet, the Jets handed the ball to fullback Matt Snell off right tackle on first down. But safety Johnny Robinson knifed through the line to tackle him a half yard short of the goal line. New York then tried Bill Mathis off right guard on second down, but this time Lanier was waiting for him. No gain.

In an October game against the Patriots, Namath faked a handoff inside and then trotted around end 4 yards for a bootleg touchdown. On third down against the Chiefs, Namath faked a handoff to Mathis into the line and then took off to his right. But the Chiefs didn't bite on the fake and instead strung Namath out to the sideline where Jim Kearney, Lanier, and Lynch all pounced on him, forcing Namath to throw the ball away. The Jets opted to settle for a game-tying field goal by Jim Turner.

Then lightning struck. On first down, Dawson hit Otis Taylor on a crossing pattern for 61 yards to the New York 19. Stram sent Gloster Richardson in to give Taylor a breather, and it became an extended breather. Richardson beat Cornell Gordon on the next play on a corner route for the go-ahead touchdown.

"That was the game," Lanier said.

In their two offensive possessions over the final ten minutes, the Jets moved to the Kansas City 16 and 14. But the first possession ended with three consecutive incompletions by Namath, turning the ball over on downs. The second possession ended with an interception by Jim Marsalis in the end zone. New York would have a final last-gasp chance to force overtime when Jerrel Wilson punted from Kansas City's end zone with forty seconds left. But Mike Battle fumbled away a fair catch at the Kansas City 40, allowing the Chiefs to escape with a 13–6 victory.

Namath finished the day 14-of-40 passing with three interceptions and no touchdowns against the AFL's best defense. He was 5-of-18 in the fourth quarter alone.

And it was on to Oakland for the Chiefs, where they would face a much hotter quarterback. Torrid, in fact. Daryle Lamonica threw a league-best thirty-four touchdowns during the regular season and a playoff-record six more in a 56–7 rout of the Houston Oilers in the other AFL semifinal. For the second time in three seasons, Lamonica was the AFL MVP.

Lamonica had been Oakland's starting quarterback for three seasons, posting a 36-4-1 record and taking the Raiders to three consecutive AFL championship games. He also owned the Chiefs, beating them five times in six tries. So Oakland had Lamonica and the home field in the 1969 AFL championship game—the final game that would ever be played between two AFL teams. What could go wrong?

The Chiefs, though, were not impressed.

"They had beaten Houston big," Lanier said. "But that didn't mean shit to us. We were much more confident for that game because we had seen the Raiders twice that year and they were both close games. After what we had done to the Jets, we had a lot of confidence in how we were playing."

Hank Stram challenged his Chiefs that week.

"Do you think they can beat us three times in one season?" Stram asked his team.

The Raiders struck first late in the first quarter, taking a 7–0 lead on a short touchdown run by Charlie Smith to cap a 66-yard drive. The Chiefs did not cross midfield against the Raiders until the final two minutes off the half, then Dawson hit Frank Pitts with a 41-yard pass to the Oakland 7. That set up a game-tying touchdown run by Wendell Hayes.

Two star players left the game in the opening minutes of the third quarter. First, Kansas City safety Johnny Robinson departed with broken ribs from a freak collision with an official on the sideline. Then Lamonica left after jamming his passing hand in the facemask of defensive end Aaron Brown.

George Blanda replaced Lamonica and took a shot at the lead on a post pattern to Warren Wells. But Wells slipped, and Emmitt Thomas intercepted the ball in the end zone. He tried to run it out but could only get back to the Oakland 5. Two plays later, the Chiefs faced a third-and-14 from their own 2. As was the case against the Jets, Otis Taylor turned in the game's biggest play with a non-touchdown catch.

Taylor beat the double coverage of Willie Brown and George Atkinson on an out pattern, and Dawson laid the pass over his shoulder at the sideline for 35 yards. That play fueled a 95-yard drive that produced the go-ahead touchdown on a 5-yard sweep of left end by Robert Holmes.

Lamonica returned and had three opportunities in the fourth quarter to tie the game. From the Kansas City 39, he threw an interception to Jim Kearney. From the Kansas City 24, he threw an interception to Jim Marsalis. And from the Kansas City 36, Lamonica threw his third and most critical interception to Emmitt Thomas. He returned it 62 yards to the Oakland 18 to set up a field goal by Jan Stenerud in the closing minutes, sealing a 17–7 victory.

"Al Davis knew they beat us twice and figured they'd beat us again," Bell said. "At that time there was only a week before the Super Bowl. So Al told all the players to 'bring your suitcases. We're going to leave here for the Super Bowl.' They all had their suitcases in the locker room. Coach Stram found out about the suitcases and made us sit on the bus after the game. When the Raiders thought we were gone, they came walking out with their suitcases."

But the only suitcases traveling to New Orleans for the Super Bowl were those of the Chiefs.

The Minnesota Vikings 31

What worked against the Kansas City Chiefs in the first Super Bowl figured to work in their favor in the fourth Super Bowl.

Familiarity.

The Chiefs had never seen the Packers in person before playing them in the first Super Bowl. But they had seen the NFL champion Minnesota Vikings before playing them in the fourth Super Bowl.

Because the merger paved the way for interleague exhibition games, the Chiefs traveled to Minnesota on the second weekend of their 1968 preseason to face the Vikings.

Minnesota was not the scourge of the NFL yet. They were coming off a 3-8-3 season in 1967, but the Purple People Eaters—ends Carl Eller and Jim Marshall and tackles Gary Larsen and Alan Page—were already in place. Mick Tingelhoff was snapping the ball on offense, and former Canadian Football League (CFL) All-Star Joe Kapp was accepting those snaps. Paul Krause was roaming the secondary looking for interceptions. The Vikings were a team on the rise in the NFL's Western Division as the Packers were starting their decline.

Kapp was 10-of-15 passing in the first half for 106 yards in that August meeting with the Chiefs and also scrambled 21 yards for a touchdown, giving the Vikings a 7–0 intermission lead. Minnesota coach Bud Grant changed quarterbacks at that point, sitting Kapp and giving Gary Cuozzo the second half. Stram stayed with his AFL All-Star quarterback Len Dawson the entire way, and the Chiefs rallied to win, 13–10.

"We played them in the preseason and beat them easily," Stram said. "We were a bigger, stronger football team."

Even though it was the preseason, the game clearly meant more to the Chiefs than it did the Vikings. Nineteen months removed from the first Super Bowl, that loss to the Packers still stung Stram.

"From the time I got there, Hank always had an edge when we played NFL competition," Willie Lanier said. "He was trying to prove we were the best, and the NFL was trying to prove you weren't."

The Vikings went on to unseat the Packers as the Central Division champion in 1968 with an 8–6 record. It was a preview of coming attractions. After falling to the New York Giants, 24–23, in the 1969 season opener, the Vikings reeled off twelve consecutive victories to capture another Central Division crown and claim the homefield advantage in the NFL playoffs. A season-ending 10–3 loss to the Atlanta Falcons was meaningless.

The Minnesota defense was suffocating, allowing a league-low 133 points. The Vikings shut out both the Bears and Lions and held four other opponents to a touchdown or less. The most points Minnesota allowed in a game after that loss to Giants was 14. The Vikings then knocked off both the Los Angeles Rams and the Cleveland Browns in the NFL playoffs in the frozen north to reach their first Super Bowl.

The New York Jets provided the AFL some legitimacy by toppling the 18-point-favorite Baltimore Colts in the third Super Bowl. But that was viewed as a fluke. Minnesota was the best team in the NFL. Kansas City was a mere second-place finisher in the AFL, technically the first "wild card" ever to reach a Super Bowl. So the Vikings were established as a 12-point favorite over the Chiefs.

But Kansas City knew something the oddsmakers didn't.

"We weren't going to lose both games," said Bobby Bell of the two Super Bowls.

As the Chiefs studied films of the Vikings, their confidence became intoxicating. Offensively, Kansas City believed it had better talent across the board than the NFL's best team.

"I was looking forward to playing them," Fred Arbanas said. "I thought we were a better team. I thought I could block their linebackers and defensive ends. Jim Tyrer was probably the best offensive tackle in football and was playing against one of his college teammates on his side (Marshall). I knew he could do the job. Ed Budde was one of the best guards who ever played the game, and I knew he could do the job. We had a helluva good team, and we knew it. We felt very confident we could beat them."

Defensively, Stram dipped into his bag of tricks for the triple stack. That meant sliding a tackle from over guard to over center. The stack part involved the three linebackers all lining up directly behind the three interior linemen. Each would be responsible for a gap along the offensive line.

"Jim Ringo was a premier center in the National Football League, and he weighed 232," Stram said. "Mick Tingelhoff was the same size. They didn't have to be that large because everyone (in the NFL) used even spacing, and there was never anybody on the nose. All the center had to do was block back, block over, or block the middle linebacker. We decided to make the center play football, so we over-shifted the line to put Buck Buchanan, who weighted 295, or Curley Culp, who weighed 270, on his nose. We felt that was the kind of mismatch we wanted."

Buchanan was a handful for bigger men like Oakland's All-Pro guard Gene Upshaw at six-five, 255, much less Tingelhoff at six-two, 237.

"I never walked out of the huddle and didn't look across the line at number 86," Upshaw said. "He was fast, quick, and strong in addition to all that size. And I had to block him. The first time I played him, he like to have killed me. I couldn't block him—I couldn't even hold him. It was never easy. I always felt if I could win 50 percent of the time against Buck, I won."

And when Buchanan wasn't on Tingelhoff's nose, Culp would be.

"Curley Culp was the best I ever saw," Oakland's Hall of Fame coach John Madden said. "I know all about Joe Klecko and Jim Burt of the Giants . . . They're terrific. But believe me, Curley Culp was the best to ever play the position."

Clearly, this wasn't the same defense the Packers saw in the Super Bowl.

"I thought we were a couple players, a couple positions short," said Johnny Robinson of the Green Bay game. "Just on defense take those five positions—two on the line, two at linebacker, and one in the secondary."

Aaron Brown at 265 pounds had replaced the 205-pound Chuck Hurston at end, and the mobile Culp replaced Andy Rice at tackle. Lanier and Jim Lynch were bigger, younger, and more mobile linebackers than Sherrill Headrick and E. J. Holub, and Jim Marsalis replaced Willie Mitchell at cornerback. Buchanan, Culp, Lanier, and Marsalis were voted to the AFL All-Star Game that season, and Brown led the Chiefs with fourteen sacks.

The Vikings were the highest scoring team in the NFL with an average of 27.1 points per game. But in Joe Namath and Daryle Lamonica, the Chiefs believed they had already beaten better quarterbacks in the AFL playoffs than Kapp. In Don Maynard and Fred Biletnikoff, the Chiefs believed they had already beaten better receivers in the AFL playoffs than Gene Washington and John Henderson. In Matt Snell and Charlie Davis, the Chiefs believed they had already beaten better running backs in the AFL playoffs than Bill Brown and Dave Osborn.

"They didn't have backs coming out of the backfield running 4.3s," Robinson said. "They had two pluggers, tough guys who would run it down your throat. But they've got to get through Buck, Aaron Brown, Jerry Mays, Willie Lanier . . . I'd love to have seen those guys playing against the Packers."

Kansas City was also playing its best defense of the season. They held Namath and the Jets without a touchdown in the AFL semifinals and then held Lamonica and the explosive Raiders to a single touchdown in the AFL championship game.

"Lenny asked us about the Vikings, and Johnny Robinson told him, 'We don't think they can score a touchdown against us,'" Bell said. "They never played against a defense like ours. And their defense had never played against our offense with those reverses."

Before the Chiefs could get to the opening kickoff, though, they would have to deal with two issues. First, Dawson was linked to a federal gambling investigation that made newspaper headlines that week. Second, Robinson suffered broken ribs and torn cartilage in the AFL championship game and was listed as doubtful to play in the Super Bowl.

The gambling story lingered all week, forcing Dawson to play the game with a cloud of uncertainty. In the following weeks, Dawson was cleared, and his good name was restored. The Chiefs weren't sure about Robinson until the morning of the game, after Hank Stram threw him some intentionally high footballs during warmups to see if he could get his arms up. He could. In Robinson's mind, though, there was no way he was going to miss playing a Super Bowl in his home state. His presence in the defensive huddle gave the Chiefs a huge boost. He was a thumper.

"We called him the Candy Man," Lanier said, "because Johnny would always lay a little sweetness on them."

The Chiefs were healthy and ready. They waited three long years for a return to this stage and the chance for redemption. And they weren't going to waste it.

"We were the bigger, stronger, and faster team," Emmitt Thomas said. "There was no doubt in my mind we were going to win if we took care of the football. We were the better team. They were a good football team—but they weren't as good as we were."

In a twist of fate, as they were leaving their hotel on the day of the game, Lamar Hunt and his wife Norma stepped into the same elevator as Vikings owner Max Winter and his wife. The four of them rode down together alone. And in silence. Winter had been awarded an AFL franchise for Minnesota but abandoned Hunt's league when the NFL came calling.

"I remember the look on his face," Hunt said. "He looked drained and very nervous. I hardly recognized him. It was one of those pregnant moments. I knew it would be our day."

And in another twist of fate, NFL Films decided to mike up a head coach on the sideline for the very first time. Hank Stram and his commentary that day would live on for decades.

The Kansas City defense made an early statement, forcing the Vikings to punt on their first two possessions. Each time, the Chiefs responded with a field goal. Remember when Mike Mercer missed a 40-yarder in the first quarter of the first Super Bowl? There would be no such misses by Stenerud in this one. He kicked a 48-yarder midway through the first quarter and a 32-yarder at the start of the second quarter for a 6–0 lead.

"Keep matriculating the ball down the field, boys," Stram told his charges into the microphone.

Robinson recovered a fumbled pass reception by John Henderson at the Minnesota 48 to end the Vikings' third possession, and another Bob Lee punt ended the fourth possession. The Chiefs started mixing in some misdirections at that point with wide receiver Frank Pitts circling right end for 19 yards.

"We had reverses to neutralize their quickness," Stram said. "Their two ends, Jim Marshall and Carl Eller, were so fast and so quick we had to do something to get them going one way and then head back the other.

So we threw the anchovy inside to give them a whiff and then went back outside."

Dawson was pecking away underneath with short, possession passes to Mike Garrett, Pitts, and Otis Taylor, completing five of his first six throws for 73 yards. The Vikings could not get the Chiefs off the field until the third possession when Dawson finally took a shot deep to Taylor, only to have safety Paul Krause pick it off.

"Minnesota always played a zone defense," Stram said. "They were very predictable. Their defensive backs played very deep, so all we tried to do was throw in front and inside of them. It was so simple it was ridiculous."

When the Chiefs got the ball back at the Minnesota 44 after the fourth Lee punt, they ran the ball four consecutive plays to set up Stenerud's third field goal of the game from 25 yards out.

"As we started playing . . . we got up 3–0, then 6–0, then 9–0," Garrett said. "We were all on the bench looking at each other and saying, 'This game is over. They can't score against us. Even if they get a last-minute touchdown, it's still only 7 points.' So we thought we had the game won by the second quarter. We were just trying to continue playing tough football. But when we got up 9–0, we felt we had won."

Following Stenerud's third field goal, the Vikings fumbled away the ensuing kickoff at their own 19. It was time to ice the game. On a third-and-goal from the Minnesota 5, Stram grabbed wide receiver Gloster Richardson and sent him in with a play.

"65 Toss Power Trap," Stram told both Richardson and his microphone. "That might pop right open, rats."

It did—Mike Garrett scooted untouched into the end zone off the left side.

"Yes, sir . . . the Mentor," Stram chortled.

"Rats," by the way, was Stram's term of endearment for his players.

The Chiefs led 16–0 at halftime, leaving a then Super Bowl-record crowd of 80,562 wondering if and when the NFL champions were going to show up.

The Vikings finally provided some offensive spark on their opening possession of the third quarter. Kapp completed all four of his passes to fuel a 69-yard drive that produced a 4-yard touchdown run by Osborn. But the exhilaration on the Minnesota sideline was short-lived.

On Kansas City's next possession, with a first down at the Minnesota 46, Dawson threw a hitch pass to Otis Taylor in front of cornerback Earsell Mackbee. Taylor shook the tackle of the closing Mackbee at the 40 and turned up field along the right sideline. Safety Karl Kassulke had the angle, but Taylor high-stepped out of his lunge at the 15 for the game-clinching touchdown.

"That's the way to inject that ball over the goal line," Stram told Taylor and his microphone on the sideline.

Taylor thus delivered the key catch in three consecutive postseason games for the Chiefs against the Jets, Raiders, and now the Vikings.

"Otis is way overdue for the Pro Football Hall of Fame," said Bobby Bell, who was a draft pick of the Vikings.

Minnesota's final three possessions of the game all ended with Kansas City interceptions by Lanier, Robinson, and Thomas—and the Chiefs walked off the Tulane Stadium field as winners of the final game ever played by an AFL team. Kansas City controlled the football for almost thirty-five minutes against the best defense in the NFL. The Vikings were a running team but managed only 67 yards on the ground and committed five turnovers.

"That was like a mugging for sixty minutes," Garrett said.

The MVP could have gone to Robinson, who recovered a fumble and intercepted a pass to key a brilliant defensive effort that held the Vikings 20 points below their season average. Instead, it went to Dawson, who survived the week-long gambling distraction to complete 12-of-17 passes for 142 yards and the touchdown.

"When I look back, my performance didn't falter that much from the first [Super Bowl]," Dawson said. "Statistically, I threw for over 200 yards (against the Packers). I had better numbers than I did in Super Bowl IV. I threw an interception against the Vikings, but it was different circumstances. They intercepted down near the goal line. Two interceptions. One in each game. But one meant the world. The other didn't mean anything."

It was a legacy game.

"I felt if we didn't beat the Vikings in that Super Bowl, the careers of

Hank and Lenny would not be viewed the way they are now," Robinson claimed. "It would have been a major disaster if we had not won Super Bowl IV. Super Bowl I would be a sore spot, but Super Bowl IV took a lot of sting out of it."

But there was still one last bit of unfinished business that the Chiefs needed to address before closing the book on the AFL chapter of their existence.

32 The Dallas Cowboys

Thanksgiving has been a football tradition in Detroit since 1934.

The Lions played their first Thanksgiving game that year against the Chicago Bears. Except for World War II, Detroit has played every Thanksgiving since then. That's eighty-six games now and counting.

In 1966 the Dallas Cowboys gave the NFL a second game on Thanksgiving, and in 1967 the Kansas City Chiefs gave the AFL its Thanksgiving "tradition." When the two leagues merged in 1970, the logical move would have been to award each league a Thanksgiving game. Instead, NFL commissioner Pete Rozelle gave both games to the NFL teams. The Lions would host the first game of the day and the Cowboys the second. For the second time in his brief football ownership, Lamar Hunt's team and league lost out in Dallas to the Cowboys and the NFL.

Seven years earlier, Hunt surrendered Dallas to the Cowboys and the NFL because it became clear that his adopted hometown was not going to support two professional football teams. Frankly, Dallas wasn't supporting either of the two start-up franchises, averaging crowds in the low twenty thousands during the three seasons they were in competition. Even though the Texans outdrew the Cowboys and won the AFL championship in 1962, Hunt moved his team to Kansas City where they became the Chiefs in 1963.

But for those three seasons the two Dallas teams competed for players, fans, and the affection of the town. In 1961, in their inaugural NFL draft, the Cowboys selected TCU defensive tackle Bob Lilly in the first round and Texas Tech linebacker E. J. Holub in the second round. The Texans drafted Holub in the first round and Lilly in the second. Holub signed early with the Texans, but Lilly's decision lingered.

"The Hunts had a Christmas party and invited me over to meet the family," Lilly said. "They were very nice. Then I met (Cowboys owner) Mr. (Clint) Murchison, and he seemed like a nice person too. But it seemed like all my close friends on Southwest Conference teams were going with the Texans—Jerry Mays, E. J. Holub, Sherrill Headrick."

Lilly was invited to play in the East-West Shrine All-Star Game in San Francisco just days after the NFL draft was conducted during Christmas week. The pressure to make a decision intensified.

"Some of the scouts were trying to give us money to sign," Lilly said. "I remember people pulling bills out of their wallets and putting them on the table. That was interesting to me. One had a big roll with $500 or $600. He went through that and then he had ones. We didn't have any money back then and it was hard to say no. But I didn't take any."

But Lilly listened—and not just to the scouts. He listened to his roommate at the East-West Game, Holub.

"He told me why he went with the Texans," Lilly said. "But I couldn't make my mind up. Finally I talked to coach Abe Martin at TCU. I told him, 'People are calling me all the time, and I'm having a hard time. I don't know what to do.' So he invited me in to visit him."

Martin had coached at TCU for eight seasons and had taken the Horned Frogs to three Cotton Bowls. Lilly went to both a Cotton Bowl and a Bluebonnet Bowl during his career with Martin.

"I don't know what to tell you, Robert," Martin said. "But I've seen a couple other teams come in here, and when they start new, they generally last about three years. In my opinion, if the money is about the same and you want to be in the area of your kinfolks and college friends, I'd probably go with the NFL. But that's just a decision you have to make."

The money was the same—$11,500. He signed with the Cowboys.

"It was based on wanting to stay around my family," Lilly said. "My grandparents were still alive, and I loved them. I had a lot of friends at TCU, and some of them went with the AFL—Jack Spikes, Arvie Martin . . . I chose the Cowboys, and sure enough after their third year the Texans announced they were moving to Kansas City. So I realized then that I made the right decision because I did want to stay around family."

There may have been a rivalry between the two leagues. Even a rivalry between the Cowboys and Texans. But not in Lilly's mind.

"I used to go have a few cool ones with the Texans because most of that team was Southwest Conference players," Lilly said. "I went out once a week with them, somewhere by SMU, for some cold drinks after practice. I kept my friendships.

"I had more friends with the Texans my first couple of years because most of the players with the Cowboys were chosen in the expansion draft. They didn't come from the colleges. So when I went to training camp that first year I found out they did not like rookies. And I'm thinking, 'I think I made a mistake.' But it turned out real well. The Cowboys are still here, and I'm still here."

In Lilly's first two seasons, the Cowboys won only nine games. The Texans won almost twice as many games (seventeen) plus that AFL championship those same two seasons. The Texans believed they were the best team in Dallas, and it frustrated them that they were the franchise that had to leave town. They craved an opportunity to play the Cowboys anytime, anywhere. But competing in two different leagues, that was never going to happen.

Until the AFL-NFL merger.

Suddenly the current Chiefs and former Texans might have a shot at the Cowboys. It almost came to pass in the first Super Bowl. But the Cowboys lost in the NFL championship to the Packers in the Cotton Bowl just hours after the Chiefs had defeated the Buffalo Bills for the AFL title.

"I pictured us there," Lilly said.

The two leagues began playing exhibition games in 1967, and the Chiefs drew six different NFL franchises over the next three summers—but not Dallas. The Chiefs avenged their first Super Bowl loss with preseason victories over the Bears, Cardinals, Falcons, Lions, Rams, and Vikings. But "Dallas" never showed up on their schedule. The Cowboys played four exhibition games against AFL teams—three against the Oilers and one against the Jets—and won them all. But "Kansas City" never showed up on their schedule.

Until 1970.

The NFL scheduled a game between the Cowboys and the defending Super Bowl champion Chiefs in the Cotton Bowl in the sixth weekend of the preseason. The Cowboys were the defending Capitol Division champions coming off a 11-2-1 season.

Four players who started for the Cowboys in 1962 were still starting in 1970: Lilly, defensive end George Andrie, linebacker Chuck Howley, and tight end Pettis Norman. There were six players who started for the 1962 Texans still starting for the 1970 Chiefs: offensive tackle Jim Tyrer, center E. J. Holub, tight end Fred Arbanas, quarterback Len Dawson, defensive end Jerry Mays, and safety Johnny Robinson.

And, of course, Hank Stram was still on the sideline. As was Tom Landry on the other sideline.

"That was a very meaningful, very significant, very emotional game for Hank and the players, many of whom were getting along in their careers," Hunt said.

Stram played all games to win, regardless of the month. He took games as seriously in August as he did in January. Since this was the penultimate game of the NFL's preseason schedule—the dress rehearsal game for the regular season—both teams figured to keep their starters on the field throughout.

The Cotton Bowl was filled that night. Neither side had to paper the house for this one. A crowd of 69,055 turned out for the long-awaited matchup between the two franchises that were born the same year in Dallas. It was the third largest crowd ever to see the Chiefs play. Kansas City won Super Bowl IV before 80,562 at Tulane Stadium and then beat the College All-Stars earlier in the summer before 69,940 at Soldier Field in Chicago.

The Cowboys were loaded. They finished first in the NFL in offense in 1969 and second in scoring. They finished third in the league in defense and allowed the fourth fewest points. The Cowboys had future Hall of Famers Lilly, Bob Hayes, Rayfield Wright, Chuck Howley, Herb Adderley, and Mel Renfro on the field plus Roger Staubach on the bench.

As the team that was run out of town, the Texans had longer memories for this game than the Cowboys.

"I'd say two-thirds of the players on the Cowboys didn't even know that [the Chiefs started in Dallas]," Lilly said. "They weren't there when the two teams were there at the same time. They were players who came later. I had nothing against the Chiefs. They drafted me, and if it weren't for the Cowboys, they would have been my team.

"But we were up for it because the Chiefs had been doing pretty well.

At that point I'm not sure how many of the old TCU players were still there. I know E.J. was still there. It was a very big deal, a very big game for us because they had won [the Super Bowl]. They had a pretty good streak of winning down through the years. They've done a good job up there [in Kansas City]."

The Chiefs played with the same passion as they did in the Super Bowl against the Vikings. It was hot—93°F at game time—but Kansas City was hotter. On the first snap of the game, Dawson hit Gloster Richardson with a 49-yard pass to the Dallas 30. On the next play, Dawson found Warren McVea for a touchdown. Before the game was two minutes in, the Chiefs were up 7–0.

The Cowboys made a brilliant goal-line stand at the close of the first quarter. Lilly and Howley stopped Wendell Hayes on a third-and-goal from the Dallas 1, then Lilly and Howley repeated the same tackle of the same player on fourth-and-goal.

That turned the ball over on downs to the Cowboys, but Dallas could not dig itself out of that hole. Ron Widby was forced to punt, but his kick went straight up in the air for 11 yards, giving the Chiefs the ball back at the Dallas 17. Four plays later, Jan Stenerud kicked an 18-yard field goal for a 10–0 lead.

Stenerud added a 44-yard field goal in the fourth quarter, and the Chiefs left the Cotton Bowl with a satisfying 13–0 victory. The Cowboys had played 204 games in the preseason, regular season, and postseason in their history, and that was only the third time they had ever been shut out. It also was the only time the Cowboys had ever been shut out at the Cotton Bowl.

"I've got the game ball from the first time the Texans and Cowboys played . . . I mean the Chiefs," Hunt said. "That was an important game to us."

There was one interception in the game—by Johnny Robinson. The Chiefs sacked Dallas quarterback Craig Morton ten times, including two by Mays. The blocking of Tyrer, Holub, and Arbanas paved the way for 129 rushing yards by the Chiefs. And Dawson threw the pass that produced the only touchdown of the game. The old Texans fared well in their first game against the Cowboys.

"It's very easy to see why the Cowboys are the winningest team over the last four years in the National Football League," said Stram in his postgame press conference. "They are a very talented, well-coached football team. I was very proud and pleased that we could beat such an excellent team."

The two teams played again in the regular season, this time in Kansas City. And this time it was the Cowboys who prevailed, 27–16. The Chiefs did not return to the Super Bowl that season, but the Cowboys did. Kansas City finished 7-5-2 and missed out on the playoffs. The Cowboys finished 10–4 and, like the Chiefs, lost in their first Super Bowl, 16–13 to the Baltimore Colts.

The Cowboys returned to the Super Bowl the following season and beat the Miami Dolphins, 24–3. They have won four more Super Bowls since then. It would be fifty years before the Chiefs returned to their next Super Bowl.

But Hunt and the Chiefs waited ten seasons to finally get a shot at the Cowboys in the Cotton Bowl. It was a moment and a victory that deserved to be savored.

Epilogue

The Dallas Texans and, later, the Kansas City Chiefs, became the winningest franchise in the history of the American Football League—just as coach Hank Stram predicted in his very first meeting with his team in its very first training camp in 1960. The franchise won the most games (eighty-seven) and the most championships (three) in AFL history.

"We played in every major game in the history of professional football and won every game—the playoffs, league championships, the Super Bowl, the College All-Star Game," Stram said. "That's a great source of satisfaction. You win with people—and our people played like their heart was a blow torch. They wore it on their sleeves. They were very emotional about what we represented in the American Football League. That was a very important part of the whole process."

When Lamar Hunt founded the AFL in 1959, his league offered opportunities for coaches, players, scouts, and cities that otherwise might never have been available to those outside the NFL's tight-knit twelve-franchise fraternity. And that opportunity was no more evident than for African American players.

Lamar Hunt's franchise hired the first African American scout (Lloyd Wells) and became the first team in either league to spend the first overall pick of a draft on an HBCU player (Buck Buchanan). Bobby Bell became the first African American linebacker ever elected to the Hall of Fame in 1983. Since then, nine African American outside linebackers have been enshrined. Willie Lanier became the first African American middle linebacker enshrined in 1986. Since then, five African American middle or inside linebackers have also been enshrined.

When the Texans won their first AFL championship in 1962, they had three Black players on the roster. In 1966, when the franchise won its second AFL championship and appeared in its first Super Bowl, the Chiefs had thirteen African American players. In 1969, when the franchise won its third AFL championship and first Super Bowl, the Chiefs had twenty Black players—half of their forty-man roster. Eleven of the twenty came from HBCU schools.

The Chiefs opened football doors for African Americans that had long been closed. When Kansas City defeated Minnesota in Super Bowl IV, its top three wide receivers (Frank Pitts, Gloster Richardson, and Otis Taylor) and three of the four starters in the secondary (Jim Kearney, Jim Marsalis, and Emmitt Thomas) were HBCU products.

Kansas City fielded one of the most underrated and underappreciated defenses of all-time. The Chiefs are the only team in Super Bowl history to lead their respective league across the board in all four of the major statistical categories—run defense, pass defense, total defense, and scoring defense. The Super Bowl also produced a sight never before seen by a pro football audience.

"Before the game, when they introduced the defense, we were eight (African Americans) strong," Hall of Fame cornerback Emmitt Thomas said.

Johnny Robinson and Thomas both led the NFL in interceptions, and safety Jim Kearney became one of only three players in NFL history to return four interceptions for touchdowns in a single season (1972). That 1969 defense produced six Hall of Famers—joining the Lombardi Packers with the most of any defense in history.

"Five of the six [Hall of Famers] just happened to be Black at a time when we as a country didn't quite know how to embrace the great quality of skill that Black people could have," Lanier said. "They didn't know how to quantify the skill that Black people could have."

It was a defense that commanded respect and admiration. One such admirer was Chuck Noll, who was beginning his Hall of Fame career as head coach of the Pittsburgh Steelers.

"That was the first great defense," said Pittsburgh's Hall of Fame defensive tackle Joe Greene. "We tried to emulate the Chiefs. We ran the KC triple stack my first three years. Several other teams tried to run it as well. That was the defense we were playing (in the 1972 AFC title game, a 21–17 loss) when the Dolphins went undefeated. I was playing over the tackle instead of over the guard.

"Obviously, we didn't play it as well as Kansas City did. We got better when we played the stunt four-three [defensive front]."

It took Stram time to collect the right pieces for his defense. Robinson arrived in 1960, Jerry Mays in 1961, Bell and Buchanan in 1963, Aaron Brown and Thomas in 1966, Lanier, Jim Lynch, and Jim Kearney in 1967, Curley Culp in 1968, and Jim Marsalis in 1969. Stram was looking for a specific trait and found it in each of them.

"Coaching is three things," Stram said. "Accumulating talent, assessing talent, and making the talent win. Look at the first part—accumulating talent. It's obvious we had talent. Second, assessing talent. It's obvious we were able to do that. We had a thousand or so players go through our camp in fifteen years, and a lot of decisions were made. And third, we never sold winning games to the players. We wanted winners. We could go downtown, get forty-five players and put them in uniform, and you'd have forty-five players. But they would never win games. We were interested in only one thing—recruiting winners."

Winning defined Stram in the AFL. He won 63.9 percent of his 140 regular-season games, 71.4 percent of his seven playoff games, and 78.4 percent of his fifty-one exhibition games. After that loss to the Packers in the first Super Bowl, Stram won eight of the next ten games he played against NFL competition while toting the AFL banner. He and Sid Gillman were the only head coaches on the sideline for all ten of the AFL seasons.

But Stram had to wait on his Hall of Fame moment—a wait that lasted twenty-six years before he was finally nominated and elected as a senior candidate in 2003. Waiting has become commonplace for the Chiefs and the AFL though. The AFL achieved parity by the end of the 1960 decade with those two Super Bowl victories, but history continues to look down on Lamar Hunt's league.

There were twenty-three position players selected first-team NFL All-Decade for the 1960s. Twenty-two of them have busts in the Pro Football Hall of Fame. There were twenty-two position players selected to the AFL's All-Time Team for the 1960s. Only ten of them have busts in the Pro Football Hall of Fame. And of those ten, three were enshrined as seniors after their twenty-five-year windows of modern-era eligibility had expired.

There were eight Packers named first-team All-Decade for the 1960s. All have busts in Canton. There were six Chiefs named to the All-Time AFL team. Only two have busts in the Hall of Fame: Bell and Robinson. And Robinson was elected as a senior.

Fred Arbanas, Ed Budde, Jerry Mays, and Jim Tyrer were all voted to the All-Time AFL team, but Arbanas, Budde, and Mays have never even had their careers discussed by the Hall's selection committee. Tyrer appeared as a finalist twice. Otis Taylor has been another omission. Lynn Swann was enshrined in Canton because of his knack for big plays in big games. That same knack by Taylor has been ignored.

"Otis Taylor was the greatest receiver ever to play the game," Mike Garrett said. "He was six-three, 215 and ran the 40 in the 4.5's. He was very physical and had great hands. At his size Otis could beat the corner down, get behind him, make the catch, and then beat him down again. He was unbelievable. And he was a mean son of a gun. It pisses me off that he isn't in the Hall of Fame. Gosh, he was a great player. He was fabulous."

Lamar Hunt brought professional football to Texas. He gave two cities, Dallas and Kansas City, their first pro football championships. And he was the one Chief who did not have to wait on the Hall of Fame. Hunt was elected the first time his name appeared on the ballot in 1972, the first original AFLer enshrined in Canton. "Games" has since been elected to ten other Halls of Fame for his contributions in business, football, soccer, and tennis.

Hunt is one of three AFL owners enshrined in Canton along with Al Davis and Ralph Wilson. Stram is one of three AFC coaches enshrined along with Weeb Ewbank and Gillman. Hall of Fame general manager Bobby Beathard also got his start in the AFL in the personnel department of the Chiefs.

Jan Stenerud was the first pure placekicker elected to the Hall of Fame in 1991. He joined Bell, Buchanan, and Lanier on the NFL's Centennial team.

"I saw the Hammer at a golf tournament recently and told him those three days turned into 19 years," Stenerud said.

The Chiefs weren't alone on the Centennial team. There were ten AFL-era players selected among the one hundred best players in NFL history. Joining the Kansas City contingent were Raiders Willie Brown, Jim Otto, Art Shell, and Gene Upshaw, Lance Alworth of the Chargers, and Ken Houston of the Oilers. Three other draft picks by Hunt's franchise—Lilly, Sayers, and Staubach—also were named to the Centennial team.

Roger Staubach owns the third-best winning percentage of any quarterback in NFL history, behind Otto Graham and Tom Brady. Despite a five-year military commitment that delayed the start of his NFL career, Staubach won 74.5 percent of his starts in an eleven-year career.

"I wanted to get him committed to the Chiefs," said Hunt, who flew to Annapolis to have dinner with Staubach after Kansas City selected him in the 16th round of the 1964 AFL draft. "My sales pitch to him was to come to the Chiefs because Dawson was kind of getting up there in years. I was trying to tell Roger that in about four years, Len would be retiring. As it turns out, Len played ten more seasons for us. We wished we'd have gotten Roger, but I'm just tickled he had the career he had."

Lanier was named the NFL's Man of the Year in 1972, and Dawson won it in 1973—an award that's name was changed in 1999 to the Walter Payton NFL Man of the Year Award. Payton himself won the honor in 1977, and another HBCU product, wide receiver Harold Carmichael, received the award in 1980. Carmichael has also joined Lanier and Payton in the Hall of Fame.

Johnny Robinson went to seven AFL All-Star Games and Pro Bowls and was a first-team All-Pro selection five times. He led the AFL in interceptions in 1966 with ten and led the NFL in 1970 with ten more. He was one of only twenty players who played all ten AFL seasons—as was his college teammate Billy Cannon. They spent Cannon's final season together in 1970 as teammates on the Chiefs. Robinson retired a year later.

"I was the last Dallas Texan," said Robinson with pride. "If the circumstances had been different, I would have liked to have been the last original American Football League player in the NFL. But (George) Blanda was still going strong at that time."

History may have forgotten the Chiefs after the 1966 Super Bowl. But they became a franchise that refused to stay forgotten again.

Acknowledgments

I moved to Kansas City from New York City in 1977. Had I not met Lamar Hunt that year, this book would never have been written. My notebooks would have been empty.

When I arrived in Kansas City, it was a one-newspaper town. Talk radio and ESPN didn't exist then, and the Chiefs were on a steep decline from their Super Bowl era. There wasn't much interest in the franchise in the late 1970s and 1980s, so the Chiefs welcomed whatever media coverage they could attract. The crowds were in the twenty to forty thousands back then—not the 73,500 that squeeze into Arrowhead Stadium these days to watch the team win Super Bowls. As a Kansas City friend once told me, "The Chiefs Kingdom used to be Luxembourg."

That gave me a unique coverage opportunity.

As a reporter, I had complete run of Arrowhead Stadium. I had open access to the locker room, training room, and coaching corridor. I used to walk down to the head coach's office in the morning and pour myself a cup of coffee out of his own personal pot. That access allowed me to develop relationships with Chiefs of the past and the present—and they had stories to tell. It was educational. I listened and learned the history of the franchise.

Lamar Hunt wore his passion for football, the Chiefs, and the AFL on his sleeve—and it was contagious. I had several lengthy sit-downs with him over my thirteen years in Kansas City, and he would regale me with tales of the early days. He was as humble a legendary figure in sports as I've ever met. Through Lamar I met his family. I used to see the Hunt boys, Clark and Dan, during summers in the 1980s running around training camp at William Jewell College. Clark is now the chairman of the Chiefs, and Dan is the president of the FC Dallas MLS team. Lamar's wife Norma even invited me to dinner with the family in Dallas when I left Kansas City in 1990 to cover the Cowboys. So my first thanks go out to the Hunt family.

All of the game details in this manuscript came from the official play-by-plays provided to me by the Chiefs and the Las Vegas Raiders. Viewing of NFL Films' highlights of the Kansas City playoff games and Super Bowls provided further depth in the game descriptions. All the quotes in this manuscript came from my own personal one-on-one interviews over the last forty-five years with the individual players, coaches, and executives. The two exceptions were the Vince Lombardi quote after Super Bowl I, which came off a quote sheet from that game, and the Stram quote after the Chiefs-Cowboys exhibition, again from the postgame quote sheet.

So many players were so generous with their time. My thanks to original Dallas Texans Fred Arbanas, Chris Burford, Walt Corey, Jerry Cornelison, Len Dawson, Sherrill Headrick, Frank Jackson, Johnny Robinson, Jack Spikes, and Hank Stram and Kansas City Chiefs Bobby Bell, Buck Buchanan, Ed Budde, Mike Garrett, Willie Lanier, Jan Stenerud, Otis Taylor, Emmitt Thomas, and Fred Williamson.

My thanks to the AFL opponents as well: Butch Byrd, Booker Edgerton, and George Saimes of the Buffalo Bills, Austin "Goose" Gonsoulin of the Denver Broncos, Miller Farr and Ken Houston of the Houston Oilers, Willie Brown, Al Davis, Dave Grayson, John Madden, and Gene Upshaw of the Oakland Raiders, and Lance Alworth of the San Diego Chargers.

My thanks to the Green Bay Packers: Herb Adderley, Willie Davis, Forrest Gregg, Jerry Kramer, Dave Robinson, and Jim Taylor, as well as NFLers Tommy Nobis of the Atlanta Falcons, Paul Wiggin of the Cleveland Browns, Bob Lilly of the Dallas Cowboys, Dick LeBeau of the Detroit Lions, and Joe Greene of the Pittsburgh Steelers.

A special thanks to Bob Moore, the historian of the Chiefs. I got to know Bob during his first year as the team's public relations director in 1989, which was my last year covering the Chiefs. We've remained friends ever since, and in his current capacity as team historian, he opened up the franchise's archives to me. If I needed a name, a phone number, a date, or a statistic, Bob could produce it in an instant. He created the Chiefs Hall of Fame at Arrowhead Stadium, which may be the finest football hall outside of Canton. The AFL Chiefs live on there. His eyes and mind were invaluable in the development of this manuscript.

I also got to know Mike Davidson in 1989. He followed head coach Marty Schottenheimer from Cleveland to Kansas City that year as equipment manager. When he retired in 2011, Mike joined Moore as associate historian and curator of the Chiefs Hall of Fame. Whenever I needed a play-by-play, a roster, or a team photo for identification purposes, Mike delivered.

The most critical research element for this book was the 2013 Kansas City Chiefs media guide—the last year the club printed an actual guide. Sadly, most NFL teams no longer print them. I spent more than five decades covering the NFL, and those press guides were always a staple in my briefcase. The 2013 Chiefs guide was not only a history of the franchise but also that of the AFL. I spent almost four months writing this book, and I opened that guide every single day. It was 588 pages of pure gold for a researcher. So a huge thanks go out to Pete Moris, who made the press guide his labor of love. He spent sixteen years building the history section and crafting the Kansas City guide into the league's best.

I also spent many a moment with the press guides of the Chicago Bears, Green Bay Packers, Minnesota Vikings, and Dallas Cowboys in researching this book. Again, it's sad to see press guides become salary-cap casualties of so many of the NFL franchises. As they disappear, the game's history disappears.

I got to know Elliot Harrison when he worked for the NFL Network. Elliot is from Dallas and one of the game's top historians. He and I served together on the NFL's Centennial committee. He knew I had this book in my notebook. Whenever he was in town and we met for fried pickles and cold beverages at Razzoo's, he'd encourage me to write it. He even loaned me his rare microcassette tape recorder so that I could transcribe some of the older interviews with Hunt, Fred Arbanas, Len Dawson, and Fred Williamson for this book. Elliot had a passion for the Chiefs and the AFL that stemmed from his father, Neal. When the two franchises started up in Dallas in 1960, Neal chose the Texans as "his" team and schooled young Elliot on the lore of Len Dawson, Abner Haynes, and Mack Lee Hill.

Kansas City public relations directors Bob Sprenger, Doug Kelly, and Gary Heise opened countless doors for me in the 1970s and 1980s as I was navigating the building and the franchise. When I was named to the Pro Football Hall of Fame selection committee in 1988, I got to know Will McDonough of the *Boston Globe*, Larry Felser of the *Buffalo News*, Dick Connor of the *Denver Post*, and Jerry Magee of the *San Diego Union-Tribune*. Their passion for the AFL reinforced my belief that the history of that league should never be forgotten.

Randy Covitz and Bob Gretz, my former teammates at the *Kansas City Star*, have always been respected sounding boards of mine. Scott Agulnek of the Dallas Cowboys, Tim Graham of *The Athletic*, Chris Jenkins of the Buffalo Bills, Will Kiss of the Las Vegas Raiders, and Dale Stram (Hank's son) were helpful when I needed a favor or an answer. Also my thanks to Mel Knowlton for that interview long ago that gave me insight into Len Dawson. And I found the Coral Reef Coffee Company in Lewisville, Texas, an ideal place to compose. Much of this book was written over coffee there.

I owe a debt of gratitude to those who carved my career path in journalism that led to this book—Richard L. Shook in Detroit, Mike Hughes and Milton Richman in New York City, Jim Weick in Kansas City, and finally Dave Smith in Dallas. They all saw something in me that at times I didn't see in myself.

And the final thanks—and the most important thank you—to my late wife Ellen. Her courage gave me courage. Her strength gave me strength. Her love gave me eternal happiness. Her spirit drove this manuscript.

Index